Miracle to Meltdown in Asia

Miracle to Meltdown in Asia

Business, Government, and Society

NORMAN FLYNN

OXFORD
UNIVERSITY PRESS

OXFORD

UNIVERSITY PRESS

Great Clarendon Street, Oxford OX2 6DP

Oxford University Press is a department of the University of Oxford.
It furthers the University's objective of excellence in research, scholarship,
and education by publishing worldwide in

Oxford New York

Athens Auckland Bangkok Bogotá Buenos Aires Calcutta
Cape Town Chennai Dar es Salaam Delhi Florence Hong Kong Istanbul
Karachi Kuala Lumpur Madrid Melbourne Mexico City Mumbai
Nairobi Paris São Paulo Singapore Taipei Tokyo Toronto Warsaw

and associated companies in Berlin Ibadan

Oxford is a registered trade mark of Oxford University Press
in the UK and in certain other countries

Published in the United States
by Oxford University Press Inc., New York

© Norman Flynn 1999

British Library Cataloguing in Publication Data

Data available

Library of Congress Cataloging in Publication Data

Flynn, Norman.
   Miracle to meltdown in Asia: business, government, and society/Norman Flynn.
      p.   cm.
   Includes index.
   1. Asia—Economic conditions—1945–   .
   2. Asia—Economic policy.
I. Title.
HC412.F56 1999   338.95—dc21   99–27812

ISBN 0–19–829552–9 (hbk.)
ISBN 0–19–829553–7 (pbk.)

10 9 8 7 6 5 4 3 2 1

Typeset by Hope Services (Abingdon) Ltd.
Printed in Great Britain
on acid-free paper by
Bookcraft Ltd
Midsomer Norton, Somerset

CONTENTS

FIGURES AND BOXES

TABLES

ABBREVIATIONS

ADB	Asian Development Bank
APEC	Asia Pacific Economic Cooperation (Forum)
ASEAN	Association of South East Asian Nations
FEER	Far East Economic Review
FDI	Foreign Direct Investment
KMT	Kuomintang (ruling party of Taiwan)
LDP	Liberal Democratic Party (Japan)
MITI	Ministry of International Trade and Industry (Japan)
OECD	Organization for Economic Cooperation and Development
PRC	People's Republic of China
TVE	Township and Village Enterprise
UMNO	United Malays National Organization
WTO	World Trade Organization

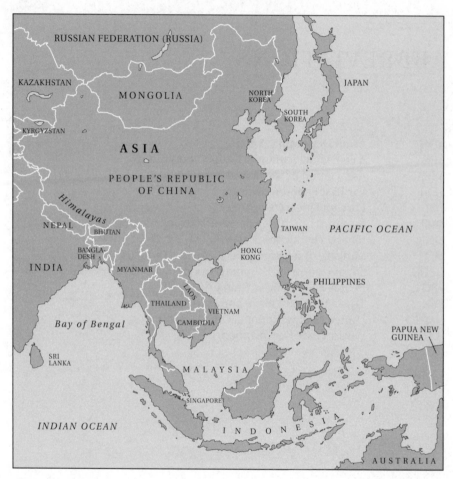

Map of the Region

Introduction

This is a book about economy, government, and society in a selection of countries in East and South-east Asia. The countries covered are extremely diverse, ranging from the People's Republic of China with the largest population in the world to Singapore, a city state with only 3,000,000 people, Japan, one of the richest countries in the world, to the Philippines with GNP per head of only $1,050. The political systems are also very diverse with multi-party democracies in Japan, Korea, and Taiwan, single-party rule in the PRC, Indonesia just emerging from a period of military and oligarchic rule, and limited democracy in Hong Kong and Singapore. The map at the front of the book should help with orientation.

Table A gives a summary of some statistics for the countries discussed. It shows that there are three groups of countries, defined by income per head. Japan, Hong Kong, and Singapore are rich by world standards, Taiwan and Korea are in a middle-income category while the rest are still relatively poor, with Thailand and Malaysia better off than the others. The countries at the bottom of the income per head league table are also those in which agriculture has a higher share of GDP. These figures are also reflected in the degree of urbanization and the number of people living in large cities. The countries at the top have a relatively low share of GDP in industry and agriculture, the rest being made up of services.

By world standards most of the countries have high levels of domestic investment. This fact will emerge as important when the question of the need for foreign investment is put. Given these high levels of domestic investment, the benefits of allowing free access to overseas investors has to be traded off against the instability and loss of control that this causes.

By European standards, government expenditure as a percentage of GDP is low, mainly because of the relatively low spending on welfare items. The comparative figures among the countries in the region are not very reliable as their coverage of spending at local level varies.

The starting point of the book is the financial crash that happened in 1997 and its aftermath in the area. The first question the book asks is whether the crash was just another financial market phenomenon or whether it revealed

Table A Summary statistics, 1995

	Population (millions)	Per capita GNP ($US)[a]	Industry as % of GDP	Agriculture as % of GDP	Gross domestic investment (% GDP)	Gov't expenditure (% GDP)	Life expectancy (male/female)	Tertiary students (% age group)[b]	GDP growth p.a. 1990–5	Urban population as % total	% Population 1m+ cities
PRC	1,200	620	48	21	40	9.4	68/71	6	12.8	30	23
Indonesia	193	980	42	17	38	16.3	62/66	10	7.6	34	13
Japan	125	39,640	38	2	29	23.8	77/83	30	1.0	78	37
Philippines	69	1,050	32	33	23	18.4	64/68	26	2.3	53	14
Thailand	58	2,740	40	11	43	16.4	67/72	19	8.4	20	11
Korea	45	9,700	43	7	37	17.6	68/76	48	7.2	81	52
Taiwan	21	12,396	36	3.6	28.7	n/a	74.9 (av)	45	6.6	n/a	n/a
Malaysia	20	3,889	32	13	41	24.7	69/74	n/a	8.7	54	6
Hong Kong	6	22,990	17	0	35	18	76/81	21	5.6	95	90
Singapore	3	26,730	36	0	33	17.7	74/79	n/a	8.7	100	95

[a] At 1995 exchange rates
[b] 1993

Sources: Asia 1998 Yearbook, Hong Kong; Far East Economic Review, World Development Report, 1997

something special about the economies in the region. The very fast economic growth in some of the countries had attracted investors and the attention of governments elsewhere looking for the secret of economic growth. There had been no general agreement about how the growth had been achieved. Was it the result of free markets and intelligent use of technology? Or was it the result of strong guidance and close partnership between governments and business? Was there some cultural foundation in beliefs and attitudes about work, savings, self-reliance, and national pride? Or was the growth achieved simply by harnessing savings and building productive capacity?

Just as there were disagreements about why growth in the region had been so fast, so there were different interpretations of what caused the crash. Some drew parallels with previous financial crashes and discounted the idea that there was anything special about this one. Others laid the blame on corruption and what became known as 'cronyism', the phenomenon of very close exclusive connections among friends and families that stopped markets from operating properly. Still others argued the opposite, that it was caused by opening up markets to outsiders without sufficient regulation to stop wild market fluctuations.

The book then goes on to examine the nature of the relationships among businesses and between business, family, and government. It is clear that the relationships are far more complicated than the simplicity of markets. Connections based on family or birthplace seem to coexist with financial and trading links. Western observers see this as a deviation from the true path of market relationships and raise the market to the highest level of ethics. Some people in the region also see the economic collapse as marking a turning point after which economies previously run through networks of connections and protected interests are finally exposed to market forces on a world scale. The book argues that the two alternative ways of organizing society, through markets and through connections, are not absolutes. First, there are power relationships in which either big and powerful companies or strong governments can impose their will on others, using power rather than market or connections. Second, markets do not operate in an anonymous and abstract way but are informed by connections and governed to some degree by the trust that arises from being from the same region or family. Third, family-type connections are not absolute either and people will try to gain advantage even from their family. What seems to be happening is not that economies that are run entirely through power and connections are switching to be dominated by open and free markets, rather that the balance between these three organizing principles or modes of governance is changing.

When the book looks in detail at the relationship between government and business in the region it shows that there is a wide range of modes of governance. At one extreme Korea seems to have developed through a very small number of powerful people building business empires through such close connections among business finance and government that the sectors have hardly been distinguishable. Similar patterns occur in the PRC where the strong party-state still has a great deal of control over finance and investment despite the development of the private sector and the market approach to the economy. It emerges that Indonesia and the Philippines also had strong connections between sectors and domination by a small clique but this did not produce the remarkable economic transformation that happened in Korea and Japan and is still happening in the PRC. Hong Kong, Singapore, and Taiwan are often referred to as the exemplars of the power of the market. In the immediate aftermath of the crisis, the Korean government has been denouncing their own history of control and connections and advocating a more free-market approach. But was it the case that the government of Taiwan simply took a hands-off approach and let the economy develop however the market dictated? Did Singapore become such a huge economic success only by the government establishing a framework of law in which the economy could operate?

Even before the crisis there could be detected a shift in the balance from planning and control by governments operating through networks of connections in all sectors towards a more inclusive and market-oriented approach together with much weaker controls. The book asks whether this is part of a worldwide process through which eventually economic and political systems will be very similar. Are there forces of 'globalization' or the exposure of national economies and societies to trade and investment and to international companies and supragovernment organizations, which will eventually homogenize the world? The strong form of this question is whether these forces will not only produce homogeneity but whether they will work towards convergence around a liberal-market model, together with some form of competitive and open politics.

Politics in the region takes a variety of forms. Chapter 5 asks whether there are any special characteristics that distinguish the region and whether there are tendencies for these characteristics to diminish and for some sort of 'liberal democracy' to take hold. Taking a medium-term historical view this seems likely: military dictatorships and autocratic regimes have been replaced in Korea, Taiwan now has contested elections, and the trend is spreading to the Philippines and Indonesia. Even in the PRC there are now real elections in the rural areas. The question is whether the political process still has distinctive characteristics even though the institutional forms of elections and national assemblies have the appearance of similarity throughout the world.

One of the rhetorical devices that has been used by politicians in the region and by some from outside it is the appeal to 'Asian values' in various spheres of life. Hard work and respect for hierarchy are called upon as explanations of economic success. Self-reliance and respect for family obligations are contrasted with a European disease of individualism combined with dependency on the state for individual welfare in times of hardship. Chapter 6 asks whether there is a special Asian approach to welfare. It looks at the growth of welfare provision, especially in Japan and Korea, and at the emergence of a social insurance system in the PRC. Are 'Asian' values sufficient to protect workers from hardship and governments from unrest in societies that have grown through industrialization and urbanization? As full employment gives way to unemployment and falling incomes, will governments have to take more action to deal with the social consequences? Certainly international bodies such as the World Bank are expressing concern about the social and political consequences of the recent crash.

Within governments, rule by a combination of personal connections and hierarchical authority has been more important than rule by merit and performance. In the sphere of management of the state, many governments have been engaged in 'reform' programmes whose urgency has been emphasized by the economic crisis. The question is whether in this sphere there are also tendencies towards homogenization or convergence. Certain approaches are common: a concern to introduce or improve recruitment and promotion by merit; and to improve the interface between government and citizens and businesses; to improve financial management. Does this mean that rule by connections is being replaced? Or are there still deep-seated beliefs and attitudes that will allow older patterns of behaviour to continue?

The book was completed at the end of 1998. At that point the aftermath of the 1997/8 crisis was still serious. Unemployment and reduced wages were still leading to civil unrest in Indonesia and to an increase in poverty in those countries that were still at relatively low levels of income per head, especially Thailand and the Philippines and also Malaysia. The PRC, Taiwan, and Hong Kong were recovering in some ways, especially in the markets and Japan was still in recession. The political consequences of the crisis were still being played out. The relatively new government of Hong Kong was subject to a lot of local criticism for its handling of the crisis. The Indonesian government was reacting to events in a characteristically authoritarian way despite having called elections for the middle of 1999. The Prime Minister of Malaysia had imprisoned his deputy and the government of the Philippines was struggling with the consequences of the economic downturn. The relatively new government in Korea found itself in conflict with the old guard and the heads of the industrial conglomerates. Elsewhere there was less instability but it was certainly too early to say that the countries in the region had recovered from the crisis and were back on their old path of economic growth.

Lessons from the Asian Crisis

In July 1997, the Thai baht collapsed. After an expensive defence by the Thai central bank, the government gave up the fight and let the currency float. Ten years of pegging to a narrow band of rates against the US dollar had come to an end. The devaluation might have been confined to Thailand if the devaluation was only a reaction to the strength of the Thai economy but other currencies followed, starting with the Philippine peso, the Indonesian rupiah, and the Malaysian ringgit. A few weeks later, the currencies of Taiwan, Korea, and Singapore were also hit. By the end of 1997, the Indonesian currency had fallen to 48 per cent of its 1996 value, the baht to 48 per cent, the Korean won to 45 per cent. The Singapore dollar and New Taiwan dollar were less badly

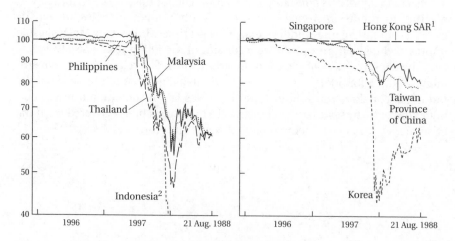

FIG. 1.1 Selected Asian economies: bilateral US dollar exchange rates

Sources: Blomberg Financial Markets, LP; International Finance Corporation; Reuters

affected, losing about 20 per cent of their 1996 values. The Indonesian currency eventually collapsed in July 1998 to 15 per cent of its 1996 value. The Hong Kong dollar and the yuan maintained their pegs to the US dollar.

The stock markets were also badly hit as investors abandoned sinking ships. By the end of 1997 the Thai stock exchange lost 90 per cent of its value, Indonesia 85 per cent, Korea 80 per cent, and Singapore 60 per cent.

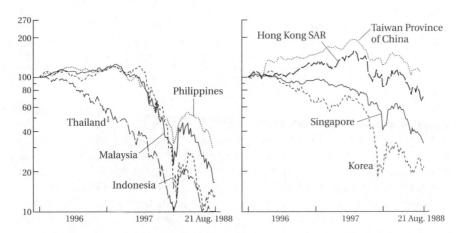

Fig. 1.2 Selected Asian economies: equity prices

Sources: Blomberg Financial Markets, LP; International Finance Corporation; Reuters

How could this happen so suddenly? Surely the whole region could not suddenly switch from being a 'buy' to being a 'sell' because the Thai banks had overstretched themselves and the property market in Bangkok collapsed? If equity and currency values reflect economic performance and profitability, they should have adjusted automatically and gradually as the fundamentals changed. The economic fundamentals had stopped being a 'miracle' some time before the sudden collapse in prices.

Before the financial crisis Western businesses were keen to invest or lend money in the region. By the middle of 1997, outstanding loans to the eight main economies in the region, excluding Japan, stood at $733 billion. The five economies that got into most trouble[1] saw a net inflow of $92.8 billion of external financing. Table 1.1 shows external financing from 1994 to 1998.

Among the optimists, the Asian Development Bank reported 'Developing Asia continues to be the fastest growing region in the world . . . overall the outlook for 1997 and 1998 is for economic growth to be similar to the performance in 1996.'[2]

Sophisticated investors and government intelligence workers must have already noticed that the Korean *chaebol*'s[3] global expansion had been financed largely by borrowing and that their balance sheets were looking weak. Hanbo Steel had already collapsed in January 1997 and Sammi Steel had

Table 1.1 External financing of Indonesia, Malaysia, Philippines, Korea, and Thailand, 1994–1998 ($bn.)

	1994	1995	1996	1997	1998
Net external financing	47.4	80.9	92.8	15.2	15.2
Direct equity flows	4.7	4.9	7.0	7.2	9.8
Portfolio flows	7.6	10.6	12.1	−11.6	−1.9
Commercial bank lending	24.0	49.5	55.5	−21.3	−14.1
Non-bank private lending	4.2	12.4	18.4	13.7	−3.3
Net official flows	7.0	3.6	−0.2	27.2	24.6
Change in reserves (− = decrease)	−5.4	−13.7	−18.3	22.7	−27.1

Source: UNCTAD, 1998: 66

posted losses every year since 1992. Japan had been in slow growth, by the standards of three previous decades, since 1989. Stagnation had affected public confidence in the government and the ruling Liberal Democratic Party was losing support. There were rumbling problems about '*tobashi*' deals under which stockbrokers guaranteed losses for clients, undermining the confidence in equity markets of those investors who did not benefit from such risk-eliminating treatment. For years the Japanese government had increased public spending without raising taxation, producing the largest accumulated government deficit of all the members of the OECD.

Indonesia's idiosyncratic political economy had hardly been hidden before the middle of 1997. President Suharto and his family made no secret of their ownership of 20 per cent of the Indonesian economy, including arcane but profitable money-spinners such as the clove monopoly. What became known as 'crony capitalism', or privileged dealings among friends and relations, had been quite acceptable while markets were up. It was only went they started to go down that investors, commentators, and overseas politicians started to take a moral stand against it.

Taiwan suffered less from these problems. There was no sign of excessive debt/equity ratios in the big companies, no sign of overwhelming bad debts in the banks. There were some strange features in the economy, such as the scale of the companies owned by the ruling party, but no cause for alarm among investors. Hong Kong had very liquid banks and conservative fiscal policy, strong domestic companies, and connections with profitable companies in still booming south China and the rest of the world. It was in fine shape. Similarly Singapore was sound, with government fiscal surpluses, good fundamentals, home of the regional headquarters of some of the most successful companies in the world, and an extremely stable government. All were hit by the wave of selling both of stocks and currency.

WHAT SORT OF 'MIRACLES'?

In the twenty-five years to 1990, output per head in East Asia grew at more than twice the rate of the OECD countries. Between 1960 and 1985 eight out of the world's twenty fastest growing countries were in Asia.[4] Between 1981 and 1990 the growth rates in the region averaged between 5 and 10 per cent per annum (see Figure 1.3). The idea of a 'miracle' was widely promoted. The World Bank published a report in 1993[5] attributing the 'miracle' to good public policies, although these varied from country to country. The fast growth rates and the increase in the region's share of world output and world trade led commentators to talk about the 'Asian Century', signalling the arrival of a new rich part of the world to rival the USA and Europe. There is no doubt that there were remarkable transformations of many economies in the region.

There was a search for explanations of these high growth rates and lessons for other countries. Explanations included good governance, good economic policy, good luck, economic intervention by governments, lack of economic

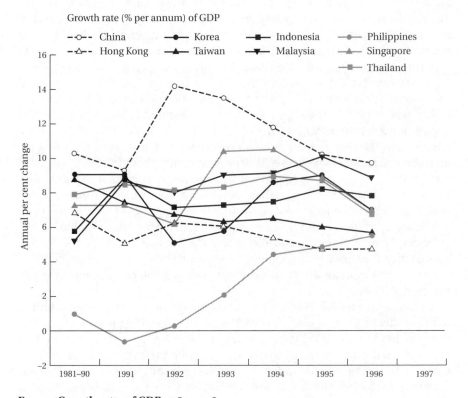

Fig. 1.3 **Growth rates of GDP, 1980–1996**
Source: IMF

intervention by governments, the impact of culture on savings, investment and the work ethic, free markets, and controlled markets. Some sought the answer in the quality of management in Japanese, Korean, or overseas Chinese companies. Some of the features of these companies were seen as virtues and possible explanations for the economic success of nations. Many of the features could be attributed to national and corporate culture, such as relationships of loyalty between employers and employees, long time-horizons for strategic planning, networks of connections among suppliers and customers, and higher levels of trust or reliance among trading partners. Whether these cultural features were satisfactory explanations of the rapid growth, they were later used by economists as diagnoses of economic problems: loyalty means it is difficult to lay off workers; long time-horizons of the *chaebol* meant they were willing to enter markets where there were no short-term profits; connections led to corruption and trust was a hindrance to more rational economic decisions. The relative strength of these opposing views will be assessed later.

The World Bank report that promoted the idea of a 'miracle' did not claim that there was a uniform set of explanations or a single path to high growth rates in the high-performing economies. It did find some common factors. The first feature was called 'getting the fundamentals right', including controlling inflation and maintaining competitive exchange rates. Effective and secure financial systems were another feature essential for channelling savings into investments with high social returns. The report was cagey about state intervention. Unable to deny that there was price distortion and directed investment it claimed that such distortions were limited and that directed credit only worked 'sometimes'. The report concluded by suggesting that the degree of management and control of the economies would be reduced as the countries in the region accepted the constraints of international agreements on trade and capital movements. What is interesting about this set of explanations is that they were presented as if there were no alternative explanations. In fact there has been a long debate between those who prefer explanations which give prominence to markets and limit the role of governments to providing a stable economic environment and those who emphasize the guidance of state planning and direction[6] The tension among a free-market approach to economic management, an approach based on close connections among sectors and the use of government planning will be a theme of the following discussions.

Explanations emphasizing 'culture' have had various elements in addition to those affecting management methods. One is a belief in the ethical foundations of hard work, loyalty, unquestioning obedience, characteristics that obviously make for a perfect workforce if they offer to their employer the tributes due to a ruler or head of family. Another is about the fundamental relationships in society. If people are concerned with the well-being of their extended family or even nation, and with future generations rather than with present consumption, this will have economic consequences in high savings

rates and long views on investment returns. It will also have social consequences in intergenerational solidarity and in the value of education as a way
of improving family fortunes not just individual earning power. These cultural
explanations bear a heavy burden. They have to apply to a wide range of countries that achieved high growth rates and a wide range of religious and philosophical beliefs, including Islam, Taoism, Christianity, Buddhism, and
pantheism, and in many cases doses of selfishness and individualism.

A more complex version of the cultural analysis of the region concerns the
specific relationships between and within businesses. Gary Hamilton, for
example,[7] looks at the networks of relationships based on obligations other
than those arising from short-term economic transactions, which have specific forms in different Asian economies. While Hamilton did not offer these
descriptions as explanations for fast growth, he emphasized the importance of
the institutional arrangements under which business is done and of the relationships between business and government to an understanding of the way
in which certain economies work. This argument goes beyond the debate
between the liberals who emphasize markets and those who emphasize the
role of the state in economic development and questions the very sharp distinction between what companies do and what governments do.

Biggart and Hamilton[8] argued that there was not a universal set of 'Asian'
organizational and management arrangements, rather each economy in the
region had a different configuration of institutional arrangements and
national economic policies and strategies. If this is the case, analysis needs to
be specific to each country rather than a search for universal attributes.

Others have emphasized the importance of the international system and
geopolitics. Singapore's government has itself spoken of the importance of a
potential threat of absorption by Malaysia as an exhortation to Singaporeans
to make Singapore economically strong. Taiwan's government has made economic growth a major defensive strategy. Japan's post-war reconstruction and
subsequent fast growth cannot be detached either from nationalism or cold-
war induced aid. The fact that the boundary between communism and capitalism runs through Korea had an impact on early South Korean development.
Indonesia and the Philippines were clearly beneficiaries of the USA's anti-
communist policy in South-east Asia.

More recently explanations have included 'governance'. Since a variety of
types of government, from dictatorships to democracies seem to have
achieved high growth rates, the argument is that there must be some common
elements in the behaviour of governments that generate growth, unrelated to
regime type. Hilton Root,[9] for example, produced a diagnosis for the Asian
Development Bank emphasizing transparency, predictability, and other
virtues in each fast-growing country in the region even during the Park regime
in Korea. This search for universal characteristics of 'governance' whatever
the type of regime is essentially prescriptive and normative. Institutions such
as the ADB are not mandated to interfere in national politics or to dictate to
national governments. They do feel able to speak of 'good governance' as

opposed to good government and produce prescriptions that avoid discussion of issues such as dictatorship and democracy.

Paul Krugman[10] was sceptical that there was any such thing as a miracle. He argued that if there are very high savings and investment rates and people are transferred from low-productivity agricultural work to manufacturing and service work, growth is inevitable and will come to an end when that transfer is complete. There is no need to explain the economic transformations other than by way of the growth of capacity. All explanations of success that emphasize efficient resource allocation and good strategies are therefore irrelevant, since the allocation of savings through intermediaries to investments was not done especially efficiently. Since adding capacity eventually means that demand is insufficient, growth inevitably comes to an end and no special explanations are required for that either.

If success was achieved mainly by adding capacity, competitive advantage did not come through technical or managerial superiority but through lower costs and the willingness to gain market share at the expense of profits. The multi-industry Korean groups such as Samsung entered product lines and markets by borrowing to build capacity in the expectation that market share could be won and then maintained and would produce profits in the long run. Expansion in low labour cost locations and within tariff walls was part of their strategy.

The editor of a report on the Salzburg Seminar expressed his difficulty in picking a set of explanations: 'In the absence of an accepted theory encompassing all of these varied factors, the best that can be done . . . is to present them . . . and await the reactions of the reader.'[11] While this candid admission on behalf of an eminent group of economists and social scientists may cause scepticism about economics and social science, it does show that there is no consensus about why there was such fast growth in the region for so long. In the absence of agreement, explanations can be chosen to support almost any proposition on how society should be run. If one believes that democracy is good for growth, one will point to the parallel growth in output and democracy in some parts of the region. If one favours authoritarianism, one can point to the opposite or the usefulness of firm government and labour discipline that come with authoritarian regimes. If one believes that the West is decadent and immoral, one can point to the different and superior ethics of the East. If one believes that free markets are the way to economic salvation, one can point to the replacement of Eastern by Western, market ethics.

The crisis presents some extra difficulties to those seeking to explain fast growth. Root, for example, has a section of his book called 'the right kind of corruption'[12] in which he explains why the corruption scandals in Korea in 1995 did not adversely affect confidence in the economy. The bribery and corruption were not detrimental to economic growth because they did not result in inefficient resource allocation. However, corruption was soon to be offered as an explanation for the growth of bad loans in Korea. In Japan, networks of linkages between MITI, the treasury, the banks, and the corporations were offered by Chalmers Johnson as a source of strength and predictability in Japan. Later these connections were revealed as an important source of poor company performance because government protection allowed mistakes and losses to be hidden.

The crisis also makes us question some of the 'cultural' explanations. Lifetime employment and mutual loyalty between employers and employees were seen as contributing to hard work, loyalty, flexibility, and productivity in Japanese and Korean corporations. When the market called for lay-offs and cost reduction such 'cultural' connections were forgotten and the relationship between employer and employee looked like a 'normal', individualistic, self-interested market relationship. Workers' responses, by protesting, in some cases by striking, also reflected an employee–employer relationship based in the market and not in some Confucian, family-type tie. If 'culture' is defined as a deeply held set of beliefs and norms of behaviour embedded in religious, philosophical, or 'national' traditions, it should not be subject to change according to economic cycles. If culture is found to change when markets turn down or competition gets stronger, then it is not so deeply embedded.

HOW DID THE 'MELTDOWN' HAPPEN?

Early signs

The usual indicator of the 'miracle', the annual growth in gross domestic product (GDP), had probably already peaked. Figure 1.3 shows the growth rates from 1980. The People's Republic of China (PRC)'s GDP growth had peaked at 14 per cent in 1992, Singapore and Thailand in 1994, Korea, Indonesia, and Malaysia in 1995. By 1996 the growth rates had declined but only back to the average levels of 1981–90. The important aspect of these rates is not that the economies of the region were growing less fast than the OECD but that the gap was closing, reducing the attraction of the region to investors and lenders who had been caught on a wave of mass optimism during the periods of very high growth.

Figure 1.4 shows the slowing of the rate of growth of merchandise exports, peaking in 1994 or 1995. Growth in exports had been one of the main reasons for and result of high levels of inward investment in the region. The dramatic drop in 1996 was an important early warning that the boom in exports was coming to an end.

These two indicators, GDP growth and export growth, viewed in 1997, may have been cyclical or may have indicated the permanent end of very high growth in GDP and exports. If the growth rates had been achieved by adding capacity and moving workers from agriculture to industry, which is essentially Krugman's argument, financing that growth from high savings rates and an

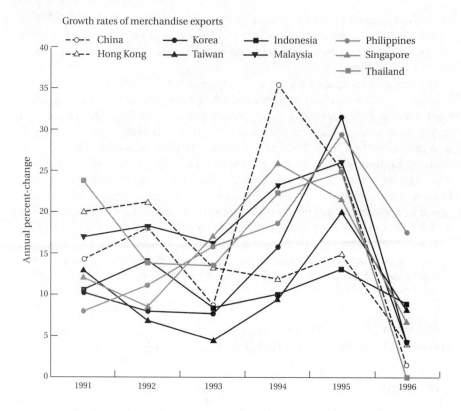

FIG. 1.4 Growth rates of merchandise exports
Source: IMF

increasing dependence on foreign investment and lending, perhaps the growth period was over.

This may have been true of those economies with high debt and no more chance of transferring workers from rural to industrial occupations and those in which high savings rates had come to an end. Table A in the Introduction showed that there are still sufficiently large numbers of rural inhabitants in PRC, Indonesia, and Thailand, at least, for employers not to have to worry about labour shortages for a long while. The other countries are now highly urbanized and will have to rely on improving the skills of existing workers, importing labour or exporting plant to where spare labour is available.

Savings rates are still higher than in other parts of the world and are still the biggest source of investment. The period of high growth may be finished if competitiveness in world markets is not restored. That depends on the whole range of items that made these economies competitive in the first place. Japan, Hong Kong, Korea, and Singapore's success has not been a result of low wages for many decades, while China and the South-east Asian economies are still attractive locations for investors seeking low-paid workers. Recovery from the fall in export growth will depend on what happens to demand in the world economy, regional exchange rates, and the ability to continue to invest successfully in the right products and markets to make profits. None of this, of course, is any different from any other economies in the world.

Speculation

Speculators make money from the change in value of a currency by gambling correctly on the rate and direction of change. People with large amounts to gamble can affect the price by placing large orders to buy or sell. Governments wanting to control the rate of change of the value of their currency can operate in the market to counter the traders. The outcome of such gambling depends on the relative holdings of the speculators and the governments (and their allies) and the skill with which each side plays the game. Partly the game is one of bluff. Neither side wants to lose all but the amount each is willing to spend is not known to the other, nor is the degree of support from friends. The hedge fund Long Term Capital Management which collapsed in September 1998 had assets of $200 billion, more than the reserves held by the government of the PRC, $120 billion at the end of 1997.

It is easier to make money by attacking a currency whose government has few reserves and few friends with deep pockets. In this case the first target was Thailand.[13] Despite an expensive defence by the government and central bank the baht's peg with the US dollar was finally abandoned on 2 July and it lost 15 per cent of its dollar value immediately.

Once a pegged currency has been attacked and devalued the confidence in the other pegs is reduced. It is harder to make money from the next victim, because there will be fewer takers of short positions in the currency. Resistance by subsequent governments makes it easier for the speculators; as long as somebody believes they will be successful, there will be someone to accept the bet. The second victim was to be the Philippine peso. The Philippine Central Bank defended the peso by buying with its dollar reserves for nine days after the collapse of the baht, after which it gave up and floated. Three days later the Malaysian Central Bank gave up its defence of the ringgit. Before the end of July the Indonesian rupiah had been hit. In September and October the wave of selling hit the new Taiwan dollar and the Hong Kong dollar. The Hong Kong authorities defended the US dollar peg and broke with tradition by also buying stocks to defend the stock market index, during 1998. The Korean won was less dramatically hit, partly because it had been allowed to devalue nearly 20 per cent since 1995 and partly because of foreign exchange restrictions.

The financial crisis had a profound effect on the real economies. The main effect was on demand: credit for trade became prohibitively expensive so exports collapsed. Government expenditures were reduced as austerity measures. The value of personal savings was seriously cut, so spending fell.

As demand fell, most of the region went into recession. The exceptions included PRC, where after discussion growth forecasts for 1998 were held at 8 per cent and Taiwan whose growth rate fell to 5.5 per cent. Elsewhere unemployment grew and output fell: the Philippines recorded 13 per cent unemployment, Hong Kong 4.5 per cent, and Japan 4.3 per cent. In 1998 GDP fell by 1.7 per cent in Japan and 6 per cent in Korea. In Indonesia, the population was plunged into poverty by unemployment and by inflation hitting the value of incomes and savings. The Indonesian government estimated in mid-1998 that over 40 per cent of the population were living below its conservatively defined poverty line. Not all of these downturns were the result only of the currency crises. As we have seen growth rates of GDP and of exports had already plunged. Competitive devaluations had some positive effects on exports. Unemployment was caused by deflated demand in the export markets and in home markets.

WHY DID IT HAPPEN?

Just as there was no consensus on the reasons for the fast growth, so explanations for the Asian financial and economic crisis are various and some are contradictory of each other. The Chinese Academy of Social Sciences,[14] for example, attributes some blame for the collapse of South Korea on deregulation. The introduction of market mechanisms in place of plans and government–business interaction produced volatility and uncertainty and increased corruption. This is opposite to the IMF's diagnosis that free markets and openness are a cure for uncertainty and volatility created by planning and government control. Financial commentators point to the unbalanced balance sheets of many companies in the countries concerned as a cause of the crisis. And yet the spectacular growth performance of, especially, Korea was achieved by using loans to create capacity—poor balance sheets were mainly a product of this growth path. Similarly, there is an argument that many of the economies were too protected from the discipline of foreign share ownership and international competition for funds. Others argue that exposure to foreign investment caused the crisis.

At a higher level of explanation for growth and decline, the close relationships between companies, governments, and banks in Japan and Korea were often seen as a cause of growth—the 'developmental state'[15] achieved growth rates and changes in economic structures which could not have been achieved by markets alone. There are those who argue exactly the opposite: that decisions made according to connections and plans are less effective and resource allocation less efficient than decisions made according to market criteria and led to the eventual collapse of those economies which were run in this way. Some people, such as Mahatir Mohamad and rioters in Indonesia, explained the crash by reference to evil foreigners conspiring to destroy whole nations, charges denied both by financial market operators such as George Soros and by Chinese shopkeepers in Indonesia whose stores were looted and bodies violated.

In other words, the choice of explanation depends very much on your starting point for thinking about what works and what does not in economic development and growth. Those in the pro-market camp will play down the contribution of planning and guided investment in the thirty years of fast growth and point to the failure to liberalize markets and reform banks. The anti-market camp will blame the crash on the uncertainties of markets and speculation.

There is no single explanation for the whole crash, unless that explanation is at the level of the whole international financial system. There was not a set of domestic features in every country affected by the collapse of stock markets and currency values. Balance sheets were in poor shape (from one perspective) in Korea and Thailand and both places had very large amounts of short-term debt but these problems did not apply to all the other countries. Thailand and Hong Kong had speculative property booms, which generated distortions in investment and savings patterns, but this was a lesser problem in the Philippines or Malaysia. There were close connections between government and business in Indonesia and Korea but this was less the case in Thailand and hardly true of Hong Kong.

The stock markets' collapses could simply be a correction in prices from an 'unrealistic' level, defined as a price level which does not reflect either earnings flows or underlying asset values. This is most likely to happen when investors are optimistic about future earnings flows or future prices. A symptom of such optimism is that the price/earnings ratios go above 'normal' levels. New entrants to stock and property markets, whether large funds or small savers, attracted by the possibility of quick gains, accelerate the rise in prices and their exit accelerates the decline.

Callum Henderson, writing about the Thai property price boom, explained the disconnection between price and fundamentals: 'if economic history teaches us two things it is that markets never learn from their mistakes (partly because the 28-year-old who gets fired for making the mistake is replaced by a 22-year-old with no experience and more importantly with no history) and also in the passionate throes of economic excess fundamentals are forgotten entirely'.[16]

Export competitiveness

While export-led growth was producing double-digit annual GDP growth rates it was considered to be a good thing. But many economies suffered loss of competitiveness in the mid-1990s. First, there was a rise in the cost of labour, first in Japan but then also in Korea and Thailand, relative to the remaining low-wage economies such as Philippines and especially PRC. Hong Kong had already ceased being a manufacturing economy by the mid-1980s, moving almost all Hong Kong owned manufacturing plants to the PRC where wage costs were dramatically lower. To some extent this also applied to Japan's direct investment in low-wage cost locations in the region (as well as Europe and the USA) and to Korean chaebol's development of manufacturing capacity overseas. Korean companies invested over $2 billion at the peak of their overseas expansion in 1994. For example, Daewoo has plants in twenty-three countries around the world.[17] Taiwanese companies also opened plants overseas, especially in neighbouring Fujian Province in PRC. Labour costs were not the only reason for building plants outside the home countries but they were a contributory factor.

The second reason for faltering export performance was the devaluation of the yen in the mid-1990s and of the yuan in 1990 and 1994 which made PRC's already competitive costs even lower. Countries whose currencies stayed pegged to the US dollar suffered from these devaluations, although they did not prevent the slowing of China's export growth.

Meanwhile there were technical and market trends against some locations. A glut in microchip production affected all producers' profitability. Footwear, a mainstay of the Thai economy, came under competitive pressure from changes in fashion and from even lower-cost locations in Asia and in Mexico.

Some economies were very open and therefore vulnerable to changes in export markets. Table 1.2 shows imports and exports as a percentage of GDP. Exposure to foreign trade is not necessarily detrimental to growth but it does make economies subject to shocks outside their own governments' macroeconomic controls. What Table 1.2 also shows is that Japan's trade exposure was less high than that of the other economies but that did not save it from a serious downturn in 1998 mainly because of falling domestic demand.

Table 1.2 Imports and exports as percentage of GDP, 1995

	Imports (US$m.)	Exports (US$m.)	GDP	As percentage of GDP	
				Imports	Exports
China	135,282	147,240	697,647	19	21
Hong Kong	192,774	173,754	143,669	134	120
Japan	419,942	494,529	5,108,540	8	10
Korea	255,834	149,446	455,476	34	33
Taiwan	121,082	126,126	260,175	47	48
Indonesia	53,244	51,160	198,079	27	26
Malaysia	86,248	81,692	85,311	101	96
Philippines	33,317	26,794	74,180	45	36
Singapore	134,028	148,394	83,695	160	177
Thailand	82,219	70,292	167,056	49	42

Sources: Asia Yearbook, 1998; Far East Economic Review, 1998

The economies were too closed (or too open) to foreign investment

One of the IMF's objectives is to create free movement of portfolio investment in and out of countries. Traders want to be able to buy and sell without government restrictions. The freedom for foreigners to buy stocks has been restricted in most Asian economies, apart from Hong Kong and Singapore. Foreign exchange dealing and overseas borrowing controls were lifted before the crisis. Korea's bid to enter the OECD had been strengthened by relaxation of government controls over external borrowing.

Capital account liberalization brought portfolio investment and loans to the region and affected the way in which business was done. The relationships between borrowers and lenders and governments during the period of fast growth were not based on strictly market criteria. Companies, banks, and government institutions accepted obligations based on connections, nationalism, or long-term sentiment. Overseas investors had different relationships with the companies they invested in or lent to. After a period of high returns and asset value growth, there was no obligation to continue to hold positions and shares were sold and loans called in. This is an explanation for the collapse only in a negative sense: had the foreign investors not been engaged in a quest for short-term returns they would not have pulled out so quickly.

Too much borrowing

If we look at some of Korea's major companies' accounts for 1996, we see that debts and liabilities as a ratio to equity are very high. One effect of this is to make the modest profits look quite respectable when expressed as a return on equity. Table 1.3 shows the accounts of seven major Korean companies.

Giant corporations like Hyundai and Samsung had very small margins and very high debts. Because of the high gearing return on equity is enough to satisfy shareholders. Hyundai Motor made a 0.8 per cent margin, Hyundai Engineering and Construction 0.4 per cent, while Samsung Corporation had margins of 0.12 per cent. The debt/equity ratios of these companies were unusually high. Table 1.3 shows the ratio of long-term debt to shareholders' equity in a selection of companies. The high debt made the companies vulnerable to the recall of those debts but also made the small margins more respectable: profits expressed as a ratio to the shareholders' equity produced an acceptable return.

This debt problem was not universal in the region. If we look at companies in Malaysia, margins were better and debt/equity ratios lower. Table 1.4 shows three of the largest Malaysian companies in 1996. There is no apparent long-term debt/equity ratio problem and margins in 1996 were healthy.

Table 1.3 Korea company accounts, 1996 (million won)

	Hyundai Motor	Hyundai E&C	Pohang	Samsung Corp	SK Telecom	LG Electronic	Samsung Electronic
Turnover	11,490,000	4,732,000	8,445,000	24,132,000	2,676,000	7,502,000	15,875,000
Net attributable profits	86,803	21,129	624,000	43,543	195,500	64,842	164,200
Assets	7,999,000	7,095,000	14,336,000	5,992,000	3,259,000	6,842,000	15,838,000
Long-term debt	2,580,000	203,100	4,313,000	1,055,000	1,404,000	2,684,000	7,330,000
Liabilities	6,330,000	6,111,000	7,682,000	4,664,000	2,201,000	5,350,000	10,749,000
Shareholders' equity	1,544,000	956,000	6,654,000	1,305,000	1,057,000	1,386,000	4,970,000
Profits as per cent of turnover	1	0	7	0	7	1	1
Profits as per cent of shareholders' equity	6	2	9	3	18	5	3
Long-term debt as per cent of equity	167	21	65	81	133	194	147
Debt + liabilities as per cent of equity	577	660	180	438	341	580	364

Table 1.4 Malaysia company accounts, 1996 (million ringgit)

	Genting	Sime Derby	Petronas
Turnover	2,596	10,780	3,898
Net attributable profits	646	693	165
Assets	6,372	26,526	1,718
Long-term debt	–	748	301
Liabilities	1,052	19,321	888
Shareholders' equity	3,672	5,527	803
Profits as per cent of turnover	25	6	4
Profits as per cent of shareholders' equity	18	13	21
Long-term debt as per cent of equity	0	14	37
Debt + liabilities as per cent of equity	29	363	148

Taiwanese companies had even better accounts. Table 1.5 shows unremarkable debt/equity ratios and respectable margins. In the case of Taiwan Semiconductor and United Microelectronics margins were over 50 per cent.

Japanese companies did not have especially troublesome debt/equity ratios, apart from Sony with a ratio of 64. Table 1.6 shows the accounts of some of the biggest Japanese corporations. Some had very small margins, such as Sony at 1.5 per cent, Matsushita 1.7 per cent, and Hitachi 1.7 per cent, reflecting the relatively flat state of the Japanese economic performance. Nintendo and Toshiba had better margins.

The accounts do not show the liquidity problems which companies accumulated as they ran up short-term debts. By December 1997, Korean companies had accumulated $160 billion of short-term debt.[18] Some company debts were spectacular, for example Kia group owed $6.2 billion when it filed for receivership in October 1997 and Samsung group owed $9.2 billion. Thailand had $90 billion in foreign debts in 1998.[19] In February 1998 the Indonesian government estimated that private companies had $23 billion of foreign debt.[20] The debts made the companies and the countries' accounts vulnerable to changes in interest rates and when they were denominated in US dollars made companies very vulnerable to currency depreciation.

Again, Taiwan was in a different position: with foreign exchange reserves at $83 billion, short-term debt was only $20 billion.[21] Singapore, Hong Kong, and the PRC also had healthy foreign exchange reserves.

What contribution did these high debt levels make to the meltdown? The answer is that the debts were not seen as a problem while companies could pay their interest and while currencies were stable. Such high levels of debt make companies very vulnerable to interest rate and exchange rate changes. Once the currencies were attacked and devalued and interest rates were increased as part of the 'rescue' packages, the debts caused both corporate and banking failures. The higher the gearing the more likely the failures. The

Table 1.5 Taiwan company accounts, 1996 (million new Taiwan dollars)

	Acer	Taiwan Semi-Conductor	Formosa Plastic	Evergreen	President	United Micro Electronics	Nan Ya	China Steel
Turnover	57,524	39,400	36,328	31,264	25,531	24,247	88,865	85,582
Net attributable profits	3,060	19,401	6,103	3,219	2,730	13,441	7,780	11,349
Assets	46,699	73,136	64,566	48,052	37,302	47,876	110,000	185,100
Long-term debt	80	5,720	1,964	5,240	3,311	5,554	7,383	11,398
Liabilities	13,715	21,022	24,509	17,142	10,851	16,009	60,438	74,434
Shareholders' equity	32,985	52,114	40,057	30,909	26,451	31,366	49,570	110,000
Profits as per cent of turnover	5	49	17	10	11	55	9	13
Profits as per cent of shareholders' equity	9	37	15	10	10	32	16	10
Long-term debt as per cent of equity	0	11	5	17	13	18	15	68
Debt + liabilities as per cent of equity	42	51	66	72	54	69	137	78

Table 1.6 Japan company accounts, 1996 (million yen)

	Sony	Toyota	Honda	Canon	Kyocera	Matsushita	Nintendo	Toshiba	Hitachi
Turnover	1,931,000	7,957,000	2,448,000	1,396,000	474,500	4,442,000	300,500	371,300	4,126,000
Net attributable profits	29,145	182,500	26,530	59,012	55,934	74,673	51,206	62,509	71,786
Assets	2,618,000	6,544,000	1,431,000	1,265,000	802,300	4,418,000	663,300	3,420,000	4,292,000
Long-term debt	814,000	526,000	213,300	95,938	50,948	623,600	–	367,900	561,900
Liabilities	1,351,000	2,196,000	669,300	485,600	207,500	2,119,000	127,900	2,351,000	2,687,000
Shareholders' equity	1,267,000	4,348,000	761,800	779,700	594,800	2,298,000	535,400	1,069,000	1,605,000
Profits as per cent of turnover	2	2	1	4	12	2	17	17	2
Profits as per cent of shareholders' equity	2	4	3	8	9	3	10	6	4
Long-term debt as per cent of equity	63	12	28	12	35	27	0	34	35
Debt + liabilities as per cent of equity	171	63	116	75	43	119	24	254	202

real question is: why did banks continue to lend to companies whose published accounts showed such vulnerable balance sheets and low profitability?

From the companies' point of view, one of the reasons for the flow of loan funds from the USA and Europe to Asia was that the cost of borrowing was lower than the rates being paid in the Asian countries. From the lenders' standpoint governments supported the loans either explicitly or implicitly and in currencies effectively pegged to the US dollar. Governments encouraged such borrowing, or at least the process of liberalization and deregulation reduced controls on overseas borrowing. The combination of cheap funds and implicit loan guarantees and continued expansion of effective demand led to the debt explosion. Liberalization led not to the discipline of the market but to irresponsibility on the part of lenders. Once the guarantees could no longer be offered, the poor judgements were exposed.

Given the high levels of domestic savings in Korea and other debtor countries, it is doubtful whether the foreign loans were necessary. It was only the difference in interest rates that made them attractive. As one commentator put it, 'money flows from countries that don't have it to countries that don't need it'.[22] In the medium term, if savings ratios hold up, investment levels may recover even if foreign investors and lenders have been scared away for a long time.

Since most of the debts were organized through banks, the crisis manifested itself in the failure of banks, especially in Thailand, Japan, and Indonesia. Bad loans within the countries and external debt denominated in dollars and not sufficiently hedged combined to destroy banks' balance sheets. It may not be sufficient to say that the crisis was a banking crisis, since these flows were only a reflection of other changes.

Just another financial crash

UNCTAD[23] points out that the Asian crisis had many similarities to previous episodes, including the Latin American debt crisis of the 1980s, the global stock-market slumps of 1987 and 1989, the European Monetary System crisis of 1992, and the Mexican crisis of 1994. Each of these incidents shared some common features. There were large flows of funds seeking arbitrage opportunities presented by interest rate differentials. Risk is reduced by the pegs of the currencies in which money is lent. Deregulation allows banks to expand into new areas of business, including businesses in which they have neither skill nor experience. Domestic currencies then tend to appreciate because of the inflow of funds which in turn adversely affects the foreign exchange balance.

Eventually, . . . the foreign balance goes out of control, and domestic financial conditions deteriorate substantially, creating vulnerability to a change in perceptions and to rises in foreign rates which can trigger a rapid outflow and eventually break the exchange rate peg, leading to capital losses on the balance sheets of banks and firms carrying unhedged foreign currency exposure.[24]

The similarity of the 1997/8 crisis to the recurrent problems in the post Bretton Woods era leads us away from specifically 'Asian' explanations of the crisis. Certainly there is nothing culturally or institutionally specific about the growth in short-term overseas debt. Table 1.7 shows the level of outstanding short-term loans in mid-1997. Part of the reason for this borrowing was to add capacity and gain market share in circumstances in which there was appearing excess capacity and reduced competitiveness. The short-term borrowing exposed firms to dangers of currency fluctuations as their ability to repay or service loans depended on making profits that could be exchanged for the currency in which the debt was held. As the currencies started to decline many firms were unable to meet their obligations and either went bankrupt or raised cash by selling their shares.

Table 1.7 Maturity distribution of lending ($m.)

	All loans		Under 1 year			
	June 1996	June 1997	June 1996	As % of total	June 1997	As % of total
Hong Kong	211,238	222,289	179,784	85	183,115	82
Indonesia	49,306	58,726	29,587	60	34,661	59
Malaysia	20,100	28,820	9,991	50	16,268	56
Philippines	10,795	14,115	5,984	55	8,293	59
Korea	88,027	103,432	62,332	71	70,182	68
Singapore	189,195	211,192	176,080	93	196,600	93
Taiwan	22,470	25,163	19,405	86	21,966	87
Thailand	69,409	69,382	47,834	69	45,567	66

Source: *UNCTAD, 1998*: 60

Some of the overseas borrowing went into real-estate development and speculation, whose collateral cover was subject to the fluctuations in real-estate markets. This added to the vulnerability of the borrowers to exchange rate fluctuations, as assets were denominated in local currencies while the loans were denominated in US dollars.

The combination of exposure to foreign debt, reduced export competitiveness because of the devaluation of the yen, and the slowdown in growth in GDP made most of the economies vulnerable to a financial crash. Once the speculation started there was a big reduction in external financing. Portfolio flows and bank lending took out $33 billion in 1997 and an estimated $16 billion in 1998 from five Asian economies, while in 1996 they had contributed $68 billion (see Table 1.1). Net external financing in these five economies dropped from $92.8 billion in 1996 to $15.2 billion in 1997.

'Asia' seems to have been defined as a single market and selling was on the basis of the charts and automatic dealing programmes rather than the fundamentals being analysed. Cash seems to have disappeared from currencies and stock markets with no thought to long-term profitability of companies or stability of currencies, their economies, or regimes.

What is the relative weight of each of these reasons for the collapse? At one level what happened in the financial markets is an explanation. Currency trades by companies and by hedge funds brought about the collapse of a series of currencies from July 1997. In a sense Mahatir Mohammed was correct when he said at the ASEAN conference that ASEAN countries were helpless victims of the flight from ASEAN currencies. Similarly the dumping of stocks caused stock-market price collapses. This does not mean that there was a conspiracy to profit from these price changes however tempting it may be for the victims to seek the perpetrators of a crime.

At a second level we need to ask how it was possible for sudden changes in prices of stocks and currencies to happen. If there are large amounts of mobile funds which can be switched from one set of assets to another, markets will be very volatile. This volatility was in contrast with some of the domestic markets: interlocking ownership among members of a group of companies in Korea or Japan and close relationships between companies and banks meant that money was less mobile within those economies and therefore the markets were less prone to sudden crash. Absence of regulation on these flows in and out of markets makes a contribution to the volatility; conversely regulation of the volumes of flow in any period reduces the range of price changes in the short term.

If this is a satisfactory explanation, the policy choice is also clear. Reduce the mobility of funds and markets will move more slowly both up and down. There have been some advocates of a temporary restriction on capital flows, including Paul Krugman and Jeffrey Sachs as well as Asian politicians. This explanation implies that prices are very detached from underlying values both of stocks and currencies. Traders are informed mainly by sentiment and expectations of price changes regardless of long-term returns. They buy in bull markets and sell in bear markets with scant regard to company profitability. Currency changes may have regard to certain published numbers such as national current account balances or foreign exchange reserve levels but these will be ignored if there is a chance to make a short-term profit on a trade.

If this is not the case, the explanation for the crash must be sought in the 'real' economies of the region. If companies' performances measured by profitability and balance sheets change, the share prices will change. If performance at an aggregated, national level is declining, then currency prices will also fall.

In the case of the 1997/8 collapse both levels of explanation seem to have some merit. The very high levels of the stock markets were based more on sentiment than underlying values. The mobility of funds accelerated the adjustment when underlying values declined and an overcorrection was very predictable.

What then is the explanation for the fact that not all currencies and stock markets collapsed to the same degree? At least two are possible. PRC and

Taiwan had sufficient foreign exchange reserves to prevent a collapse of the yuan and the new Taiwan dollar. In both cases there were regulations in place to prevent uncontrolled inward investments, especially portfolio investment. While the PRC has high levels of foreign investment it does not have very liquid stock markets nor does the government allow uncontrolled investments whether through share purchase, direct investment, or acquisitions. Taiwan had rules about the proportion of company stock that can be owned by foreigners. Both territories had high foreign exchange reserves and low levels of external debt.

But if we look at their performance in GDP growth and rate of growth of exports (see Figures 1.3 and 1.4), the PRC was performing best in the region on GDP growth but export growth fell with the rest. Taiwan's GDP and export growth performance is no different from the rest of the region.

RESPONSES

IMF

The three governments which had to borrow from the IMF sent 'letters of intent'[25] setting out their programme which they offered in exchange for the loans. They were concerned almost exclusively with deregulation and privatization and with a conservative fiscal policy and tight monetary policy. These two sets of solutions implied that the problems were caused by microeconomic structural conditions of regulation and market structure and loose macroeconomic policies. Neither explanation was especially strong.

Thailand's letter detailed a cut in public spending of 100 billion baht, or just under 2 per cent of GDP, and increases in tax on alcohol and tobacco and cars and luxury goods in order to make a fiscal surplus of 1 per cent of GDP. Indonesia also made a plan in November 1997 to create a fiscal surplus of 1 per cent of GDP but abandoned the idea by January 1998 as not possible politically. Korea, in its policies announced for the standby arrangement in December, announced that it would aim for a balanced budget or a small surplus for 1998.

Monetary policy in all three cases consisted of increasing interest rates, as part of a general tightening of credit. This had the effect of accelerating the recession and making it more likely that companies would become insolvent. Increased interest rates had little or no effect on defending currency values.

One of the main elements of the letters of intent was about restructuring the financial systems, mainly closing banks that were making losses and improving supervision and regulation. It may be surprising that these things were not done before, but only if one believes that banks should always operate as profit-maximizing businesses. In Korea the banks had been an instrument of industrial policy, in Indonesia an easy way for friends and relatives of the

President to make money, and in Thailand a useful source of credit mainly for property speculation. The crisis was certainly a threat to foreign creditors and the measures allowed them to be protected.

Thailand and Indonesia announced privatization measures which probably would not have been taken without IMF intervention. The Thai government's letter of intent included a commitment to reduce the government's stake in Thai Airways and Bangchak petroleum company and to privatize other state enterprises not yet corporatized.[26] Indonesia's letter of intent established a Privatization Board and pledged to privatize twelve enterprises in the first year and to reduce the government's holdings in other enterprises.

The social policies that the IMF claimed it was following in all its interventions[27] were less clear than these privatization promises. For example, Thailand limited the increase in the minimum wage to 2–3 per cent for 1998. 'Given the sharper-than-expected impact on the domestic economy of the adjustment process,' it was announced, 'the government is determined to accelerate the implementation of plans to protect the weaker sections of society. Thus, we expect the Asian Development Bank to move speedily and announce a social sector support programme by early 1998.'[28] Indonesia included a section on the 'Social Safety Net'. This consisted of a community-based work programme in rural areas and an expansion of the programme for the least developed villages. They also announced they would increase health and education spending from 1999. Korea's letter had nothing on privatization or social policy.

There were also changes in rules about foreign ownership. Korea raised the limit on foreign ownership of listed Korean shares from 26 to 50 per cent, removed the ceiling on foreign investment in Korean equities, and raised the ceiling on bond holdings. Thailand announced full liberalization of foreign equity investment in the financial sector. Indonesia announced that it would reduce its list of activities prohibited to foreign investors.

Indonesia and Korea announced trade liberalization measures. Indonesia promised to phase out export taxes and quotas and import restrictions. Korea promised steps to open up to imports and to eliminate trade-related subsidies.

Until the 1997/8 crisis it was possible to argue that governments in the region did not have to take too much notice of intergovernmental or supranational organizations. The crisis showed that policy independence derives in part from financial health. However, there are still reasons to be cautious about the power of the IMF. First, countries which did not have to borrow from the IMF, such as Japan, also made structural changes and tightened up banking regulation. They did this because of the obvious dangers of long-term bad debts and unwise lending. Second, it was not necessarily the case that governments did what they promised the IMF. The experience in Indonesia was that even a desperate government in poor financial condition could be strong enough to resist IMF pressure in some areas, such as privatization.

The crisis provoked political responses which removed the governments of Japan and Indonesia and contributed to Mahatir's conflict with his deputy, Anwar Mohammed in Malaysia. The run-up to the crisis also contributed to the election of Kim Dae Jung in Korea. It is not obvious that the crisis had anything to do with the replacement of the government in the Philippines, whose president was constitutionally unable to stand for another term. The politics of the crisis will be discussed further in Chapter 5.

LESSONS

At the end of 1998 the recovery from the crisis was patchy. Indonesia was forecast to have a further 3.4 per cent drop in GDP for 1999, Malaysia, Thailand, and South Korea were expected to see declines in GDP and very weak domestic demand. Taiwan and PRC were forecast to have slightly slower growth than in 1998, Japan to remain in recession, the Philippines to grow slightly and Singapore to have zero growth.[29] Indonesia was still the site of riots and unrest, 7,000,000 people were still out of work in Thailand, and Hong Kong had its highest unemployment rate ever. Stock markets had largely stabilized as had the currencies, albeit at lower levels than before the crisis.

Clearly the 1997/8 crash was severe for most of the region and the financial crisis had a deep impact on many real economies. This chapter has shown that explanations for the crisis are many and varied, as were explanations for the 'miracle' years, but there are some conclusions that can be safely made.

The volume of funds involved in the currency and stock-market crashes was large with respect to the size of the economies the funds were invested in. The relatively disconnected funds looking for returns are a source of market instability, whatever the relationships between the trades and the economic fundamentals. This applies mainly to international funds but there are also signs that domestic investors in the region treat their investments as short-term speculations.

The second conclusion is that there were large differences in economic performance in the region and while this did not affect the degree to which currency and stock speculation occurred it did have an effect on the depth of the crisis and the speed of the recovery. Thailand, Indonesia, and Korea were worst affected while PRC and Taiwan were least badly hit.

A third conclusion is that the international response to currency crises needs to be more sensitive to the nature and causes of economic problems and their social consequences. The measures described in the 'letters of intent' were not the best policies for the affected countries. In particular, they failed to deal with the question of inadequate domestic demand and included polices that made matters worse. The World Bank has recognized this, even if the IMF continues to defend its position. Dipak Dasgupta, a principal economist at the Bank, said in December 1998[30] that some of the initial policy responses, such as sharp interest-rate rises to stabilize currencies, had not worked and had exacerbated negative impacts on the real economy. He also said the severity of the crisis had been severely underestimated. 'If this crisis was very different, then the correct policy responses to deal with the crisis were probably very different—and that was underestimated,' he said. 'Policies to deal with those who were hurt most should have been much more central in the design of the macroeconomic policy response.' Dasgupta said the primary focus now should be to work on restoring domestic demand and expanding social safety nets.

It may be the case that 1998 marked a turning point in the way in which the economies of the region are run. The following chapters look at the economic structures, political processes, government and welfare systems in the region to see whether there are any common features that may characterize the region. Many governments in the region are engaged in what they call 'reform' processes designed to make the economies more open, to reduce the connections between government and business, and to create more visible and accountable markets. Only in the case of Hong Kong where the government has started taking stock positions to stabilize the markets has the move been towards more rather than less government involvement in the economy. This may mean that there is a general trend away from the previous governance mechanisms that have been apparent in many countries of the region, in which close connections between government, financial institutions, and business have been the norm. The next chapter addresses the question of the nature of relationships and organizational boundaries that exist in East and South-east Asian societies.

NOTES

1. Indonesia, Malaysia, Philippines, Korea, and Thailand.
2. Asian Development Bank, *Asian Development Outlook 1997 and 1998* (Hong Kong: OUP, 1997): iii.
3. '*Chaebol*' is a Korean word for industrial conglomerate.
4. The countries with the top twenty growth rates during this period also included Botswana, Malta, Egypt, and Brazil. Because seven of the top eight were in Asia, the 'miracle' label did not include the other high performers.
5. World Bank, *The East Asian Economic Miracle* (New York: OUP, 1993).
6. For an account of the dispute, see R. Wade, 'Japan, the World Bank, and the Art of Paradigm Maintenance; The East Asian Miracle in Political Perspective', *New Left Review* (1996): 217.
7. G. Hamilton (ed.), *Asian Business Networks* (Berlin, New York: Walter de Gruyter, 1996) and G. Hamilton, 'Organization and Market Processes in Taiwan's Capitalist Economy', in M. Orrù, N. W. Biggart, and G. Hamilton, *The Economic Organization of East Asian Capitalism* (Thousand Oaks: Sage, 1997).
8. N. W. Biggart and G. Hamilton, 'On the Limits of Firm-based Theory to Explain

Business Networks: The Western Bias of Neo-Classical Economics', in *The Economic Organization of East Asian Capitalism*.

9. H. L. Root, *Small Countries, Big Lessons* (Oxford: OUP, 1996).
10. P. Krugman, 'The Myth of Asia's Miracle', *Foreign Affairs* (Nov. 1994).
11. H. S. Rowan (ed.), *Behind East Asian Growth: The Political and Social Foundations of Prosperity* (London: Routledge, 1998): 5.
12. Root, *Small Countries, Big Lessons*: 163.
13. For an account of the game in detail see C. Henderson, *Asia Falling?* (Singapore: McGraw-Hill; US edn. title: *Asia Falling*, 1998): 98–143.
14. Conference presentation, Beijing, Aug. 1998.
15. See e.g. Chalmers Johnson, *Japan: Who Governs? The Rise of the Developmental State* (New York: Norton, 1995) and the discussion in Ch. 3.
16. Henderson, *Asia Falling?*: 94.
17. See G. R. Ungson, R. M. Steers, and S.-H. Park, *Korean Enterprise: The Quest for Globalization* (Boston: Harvard Business School Press, 1997): 37.
18. *Korean Economic Weekly*, 9 Feb. 1998.
19. IMF statement, 12 Feb. 1998.
20. Announcement at Council for the Consolidation of Economic and Financial Resilience, 6 Feb. 1998.
21. Reuters News Service, 5 Feb. 1998.
22. Brian Reading, *Financial Times*, 20 Dec. 1997.
23. United Nations Conference on Trade and Development, *Trade and Development Report, 1998* (Geneva: United Nations, 1998).
24. Ibid. 58.
25. Available on IMF's homepage at www.imf.org.
26. It is normal for state enterprises to be 'corporatized' prior to privatization: they have separate accounts and are managed relatively independently of government.
27. An extract of a speech by Mr Camdessus, managing director of the IMF, that sets out official policy is in Ch. 4.
28. Letter of intent, 25 Nov. 1997.
29. *Asia Pulse*, Singapore, 10 Dec. 1998.
30. *Business Day*, Thailand, 4 Dec. 1998.

Expressive Relationships and Networks

CHALLENGED ASSUMPTIONS

The relationships between the economy and politics or between the state and business in East and South-east Asia present some challenges to standard Western ways of thinking. The norm in the West is that there *should* be a very clear distinction between government and business and if government ministers are involved in business this means that they are corrupt. The fact that the families of prime ministers and presidents benefit from contracts with government is something to be ashamed of and has been called 'cronyism' in the Western press. Similarly people who proclaim the virtues of the market are sceptical of governments planning economic development and directing investment and credit. It is assumed that individuals acting according to economic rationality will produce better results than collective action taken according to criteria other than profit and that dealings among groups of family members will not produce optimal resource allocation.

Such an attitude shows characteristics of what Edward Said called 'orientalism',[1] that is defining societies that are not in the West negatively in relation to the categories and relationships that seem to exist in the West. In this case if a family has one member appointed as, say, provincial governor and another is president of the provincial bank, the relationship may be described as *not ethical* by standards which come from outside that society. This can extend to relationships within and between businesses. Preferential treatment for a member of a conglomerate may be seen as unethical by the standards of individualism and profit maximization, standards which may not be applied by the people in that business relationship. The relationships are not defined according to what they *are*, for example familial, but according to what they are *not*.

Some examples will illustrate the point. The fifteenth Party Congress in the PRC announced that the People's Liberation Army (PLA) was not to be allowed to acquire any more business interests. There are not many armies in the world, which are officially allowed to operate as profit centres to generate revenues to subsidize their defence and internal security operations. The fact that the army has major investments in many countries, including the USA, and is a large trading organization challenges the standard view that armies are funded by taxation and work for national governments, albeit that they sometimes take over governments.

People in the West do not normally think of armies as corporations. After all, if the army becomes financially independent of its government, there are quite serious constitutional implications. It could be imagined, for example, that the generals would disobey orders that were bad for business. In fact the PLA's entrepreneurial efforts began during the economic reform which encouraged all state bodies to find sources of revenue other than taxation. The reason that the policy of self-sufficiency arose was that in China at the time there was a different definition of 'state' and 'non-state'. When a majority of industrial and commercial enterprises are state-owned, the boundary between state and business is not at all clear. If there is a policy that state-run institutions such as hospitals, welfare homes, and schools should become more financially self-reliant by establishing commercial operations, then why should the armed forces be excluded? The PLA is not the only institution that has had its goals distorted by the requirement to make money. Social welfare institutions have also started ventures completely outside their mandates, which have claimed the attention of their managers and diverted attention away from the main goals. The Communist Party would now rather have the army under its financial control in a more conventional relationship with the party-state.

Logging concessions in Malaysia have been routinely handed out by state governments to the relatives of the state premiers.[2] The rights used to switch to the new incumbent's family when somebody else got elected. Of course politicians do favours for their relatives and supporters and business people do not give money to politicians out of altruism or generosity in most societies. The practice has recently been condemned in Malaysia as corruption but for a long time it was accepted that election to government brought with it the right to enrich one's family. Perhaps such attitudes are a remnant of the colonial period during which the distinction between the occupying forces and the companies exploiting natural resources was very blurred and the purpose of colonial rule was to enrich the colonizers.

The Kuomintang (KMT), the party that ruled Taiwan almost unopposed for forty years, owns a group of significant businesses whose profits finance the party and whose activities can be used to increase the party's support and influence. State enterprises are a normal part of economic life, albeit a shrinking sector, especially those formed for purposes of spreading risk and accelerating economic development when there were no large private corporations. It may be perfectly acceptable for major corporations to make donations to parties and presidential campaign funds but the idea of a political party owning large parts of the economy seems odd to a Western observer. It is even more surprising that the party managed to keep the holdings undisclosed until the mid-1990s.

The financial collapse in Japan in late 1997 revealed to the rest of the world some things which Japanese people had always known. For example, the scandal of losses by housing finance cooperatives (*jusen*) being financed by the Ministry of Finance to the tune of $8 billion, when those cooperatives were largely run by ex-Ministry of Finance civil servants. This seemed different from the savings and loan collapse in the USA in which the 'Savings and Loans' were caught by the change in interest rates making the relationship between short-term debts and long-term loans economically non-viable. In Japan the Ministry of Finance insider group was merely looking after its members. Existing officials could reasonably expect eventually to become *jusen* executives and in any case form part of a unified bureaucratic élite. Some Western observers describe these relationships simply as corrupt.

When the Japanese government announced that it wanted to privatize the post office savings bank it became more widely known that the bank had deposits totalling four times as much as the world's biggest bank, Tokyo-Mitsubishi. When the financial crisis hit, savers increased their deposits in the post office bank in preference to the private banks because they had more confidence and deposits grew even more, to Y244.8 trillion.[3] This also challenged certain assumptions about the trust the population had in a state-run institution and about the boundary between the state and the banks.

The example of welfare provision in Hong Kong shows that a large proportion of the finance is derived from the Hong Kong Jockey Club, a not-for-profit organization that organizes horse racing and gambling on horse racing and numbers, the 'Mark Six' lottery. The Jockey Club builds old people's homes, schools, university buildings, and medical clinics. The Jockey Club's contribution consists both of a tax on gambling and the profits made from gambling operations. A committee disburses the funds. There are foundations in other countries with similar functions, distributing funds to worthy causes and many countries have national or provincial lotteries raising money for charitable purposes. What is different about the Jockey Club is that it has a state-enforced monopoly on gambling in Hong Kong. It is a privately run charitable institution, operating a state monopoly for charitable purposes.

More than these individual jolts to preconceptions about particular institutions and events, the facts of life in East and South-east Asia challenge the basic categories with which one thinks about society. It is of course well known that businesses influence governments and that in one-party states the distinction between the party and the government is blurred and that in many places politicians are 'corrupt', in that they sell favours and buy votes with the proceeds. These events are considered deviant from a norm that *should* be followed rather than part of an alternative set of norms.

Even within the business sector, in Korea it has become apparent since the crisis that the over-borrowing by the corporations (the *chaebol*) was not just condoned by over-lending banks. The network of connections among the

banking and the industrial and commercial sectors was in effect people lending to themselves or to people to whom they were very closely connected. The
election of Kim Dae Jung, an outsider, seemed a challenge to these connections which had controlled the economy for decades. The challenge was
finally made when Kim called the leaders of the five biggest business groups to
the 'Blue House', the President's residence, in December 1998 to tell them to
sell off half their subsidiaries to reduce the size of their business empires.

The political factions in Japan were as closely connected to their factions'
pieces of the state apparatus they had captured and held under their control
as they were to any constituency outside the state apparatus. A faction within
the LDP and its network of institutions could be as powerful in its effect on
economic policy as the formal apparatus of government.

In the PRC factions connecting ministries, enterprises, the Bank, and
provincial governments determine what policies will be implemented. Policy
change in the PRC is a process of establishing acceptance and consensus
among a variety of factions and interests which cross Western boundaries of
state, party, and business.

The close ties between business and the state, whether through family or
party networks (or both together), cannot adequately be described if the organizations are seen as separate. Moon and Prasad have argued that, in the cases
of Japan and Korea, the affiliations outside the official relationships form 'a
dense and multiple network of affiliations'.[4] Chapter 3 shows that civil servants are far from a detached technocracy that takes care of the state's role in
economic development. There are connections which make the state institutions far from independent of business. There may be an organization called
the 'Ministry of Finance' but what matters is that the people who run it have
strong ties with another organization called a housing loan cooperative. The
connection between the two may be more important than the fact that they
are legally independent of each other. In Taiwan the connection between the
KMT and its clients whom it has controlled and influenced over the years is an
important explanation of the development of the economy and politics. The
idea of political parties as distinct entities competing for votes for the right to
manage the state had no bearing on Taiwan during the whole of its period of
rapid growth.

Systematic familial and personal connections between the institutions of
the state (civil service, army, police, judiciary, education system) and the institutions of the economy (banks, corporations, small and medium-sized businesses) or between the state and 'civil society' (trade unions, trade
associations, churches) lead one to realize that perhaps the connections are
more important than the boundaries.

In the case of the state and the family, Western notions of the exchange of
rights and obligations, which characterize the relationship between the state
and the individual in an idealized liberal democracy, do not necessarily apply
elsewhere. In Chapter 6 we see that the relationship between families and
the state are rarely 'contractarian' in the sense that government accepts

obligations to discharge rights of access to a standard of living as part of citizenship.

There are people[5] who argue that the reason for this lack of rights and obligations lies in a different attitude to rights and obligations. Whether 'Confucian' values of virtue underlie people's attitudes or whether they are used by politicians as excuses for spending little on substituting for family care, many states have survived without any obligation to guarantee the welfare of their citizens. In any case the idea of 'virtue' in an action such as giving care to a stranger does not imply that the giver of the care has an obligation nor that the stranger has a right to it. The notion of virtue does not imply a contract and this may be another example of 'Western' people asking the wrong questions about 'Eastern' societies. To ask a question about the absence of a state obligation for the welfare of its citizens is to imply that such an obligation should or at least might exist.

Two approaches to this problem are possible. One is to maintain a Western perspective and assume that what is Western is 'advanced' and that the rest of the world will eventually converge. If the world is converging on a social system of market domination, democracy, and the rule of law, then all social relations that deviate from these principles are anachronistic and will eventually be swept away on the tide of globalization and homogenization. It is therefore reasonable to define relationships as 'not ruled by market principles', or 'not democratic' (and therefore authoritarian, despotic, etc.), or 'not governed by the rule of law'. The negatives imply that the relationships are temporary. 'Rule by connections' in which obligations are defined according to an individual's relationships with others could also be seen as an aberration from rule by markets and democracy.

Alternatively, we could look for the actually existing relationships. After all, only an economist would look for economic self-interest in every single relationship and see every exception as deviant. If we find, for example, that a relationship between two entities is based on family ties, we could define it as an 'irrational' relationship from the viewpoint of self-interest or we could accept it for what it is, an expression of obligations which arise outside the framework of individual self-interest. The rest of this chapter defines some of the forms of relationship that do not rely on a narrow view of motivation.

EXPRESSIVE AND INSTRUMENTAL TIES

In practice there may be mixtures of 'economic rationalism'[6] and relationships founded on other grounds. The first distinction we need to make is between 'expressive' and 'instrumental' ties between individuals. An instrumental tie is one in which the relationship exists only for the purposes of the particular transaction and both parties enter the relationship only to gain advantage from it. A trading relationship, for example, is one in which a buyer and a seller trade with each other because both feel that they can get an advantage. An employment relationship is one in which the worker sells her time and skill for money and the employer believes she can profit from it. The self-interest may be complicated: two people may want to maintain a harmonious trading relationship by not profiting from absolutely every trade. An employer may wish to retain employees by not making as much profit as possible from them in the short term. An instrumental relationship does not necessarily imply that each side wants to maximize short-term gains but it is still a relationship entered for benefit.

An expressive tie is one in which the obligations between two individuals arise not from the transaction in which they are currently engaged but from their previously defined relationship. A trading relationship between two brothers might imply disclosure of information from one to the other that would not be disclosed between strangers. A traditional example from China was that debts among family members would be deemed to be written off after the next lunar New Year. One important aspect of expressive ties is that there are obligations which arise from a shared understanding of the relationship which does not have to be renegotiated each time two people deal with each other. There is limited scope to choose expressive ties: while someone can choose whether to honour the relationships, they cannot choose their parents.

There are people who say that societies based on traditional relationships are doomed to remain poor. Because people do not buy at the best possible price but rather from their relatives, overall economic efficiency is reduced. Development requires that people behave according to economic rationality rather than 'sentiment'. 'Modernization' theorists would say that in an economy consisting of transactions based on trust, resources will be allocated inefficiently and growth will be slower than its potential. Investments will be made in the wrong businesses and loans made to the wrong borrowers.

There is another possibility, which is that trust based on such obligations is faster and cheaper to acquire than trust based on a long series of observations and that such transactions may indeed be optimal. A 'culturalist' argument is that 'tradition and modernity not only coexist, but penetrate and intermingle with one another'. Far from being an obstacle to development 'tradition is seen by the culturalists as highly beneficial to development'.[7] In this argument, the traditional relationships are a help, not a hindrance to economic development. This book asks whether culture can be both a help and a hindrance to development: in the short term can such relationships speed growth by reducing transaction costs? In the long term can the networks formed from such relationships produce economic crisis or slower growth?

An alternative proposition is that a transaction guided, at least in part, by considerations other than profit may produce results beyond profit and which may be more valuable to the participants than profit. For example, a transaction may take place between firms owned by members of the same family, even if both firms might benefit more from trading with someone else, because such a transaction contributes to the coherence of the family, rather than the individual members' wealth. The family might define its own well-being as its coherence and solidarity rather than its wealth.

Such an argument might be extended to a nation. If people believe that the development of their nation is more important than individual wealth, they may be willing to sacrifice the benefits of cheaper imports in order to foster national development. In the long run such sentiment could be erroneous, if theories of comparative advantage are correct. People may feel that they are benefiting national development by buying local products rather than imports but in fact they are simply delaying the process of economic adjustment that would enable local producers to switch to making those products in which there is a local comparative advantage.

Import restrictions may be imposed to safeguard the interests of particular sections of society rather than the nation as a whole. Rice growers and other farmers in Japan are a source of political support for the LDP and restricting rice imports operates to the detriment of rice-eaters.

Liberalization of trade attacks both of these strategies, whether the short-term interest of the nation as a whole or the long-term interests of the beneficiaries of protection. Trade liberalization is an important case of substituting economic rationality for other types of relationship.

If people had held the belief that short-term economic rationality is the only decision criterion, the phase of import substitution which Korea's growth went through or the phase of import restriction which Japan organized might never have happened. The argument has now moved on to capital flows and whether investments should be allowed to cross boundaries according to price and return without control or regulation.

A fourth proposition is that transactions among family members lower transaction costs because of the degree of trust between the participants in the transaction.[8] If you can trade with a member of your family, you do not have to go through elaborate processes of checking creditworthiness or reliability, since the obligations that you have to each other as family members will ensure that neither cheats. Such a transaction would satisfy the criterion of economic rationality on the grounds of profit maximization if the gains from lower transaction costs outweigh the losses from paying a higher price.

The same applies to the development of high-reliance relationships in a long series of transactions, which also reduces transaction costs.[9] Frequent exchanges and the development of mutual reliance through contacts outside the formal transactions may develop obligations that would be broken by acting out of pure self-interest. In turn, these obligations reduce transaction costs and may improve economic efficiency, even if on occasion the prices agreed might be higher than those in a consecutive series of competitive transactions. In principle the two cases are different: the development of high-reliance relationships through a series of transactions that has gone well for both partners is different from a high-trust relationship that is based on membership of a common family, province, or class of graduates. The latter trust relationship can never be developed without the previously existing relationship.

A hierarchy can also contain elements of relationship beyond giving and accepting instructions. As in other transactions, repeated experience of instructions carried out can reduce the detail of the instructions and the need for supervision. Similarly, obligations arising from outside the hierarchy may affect the degree to which instructions are complied with. This means that instrumental relationships do not necessarily follow strict market or hierarchical rules.

The 'expressive' part of the relationship is not a simple one. Fei Xiatong,[10] the Chinese sociologist and anthropologist, offered one approach to the complexity of the expressive relationship. His observation and analysis of the relationships in the village he studied offer a good starting point for understanding relationships in business and among other networks in societies in which expressive relationships exist. Expressive ties have several features. Each link in a Chinese person's network is defined in terms of a dyadic social tie (*gang*). These interpersonal ties are known as *guangxi*. Each one has its own rules and rituals understood by both members. The ties can come from the relationships within a family and between rulers and ruled but these are not the only forms of *guangxi*. The relationships among classmates still form important obligations in both Chinese and Japanese societies. Place of birth is another important source of *guangxi*. Such ties can extend through generations who share ancestors' birthplace rather than a shared experience of being brought up in the same location.

The importance of these relationships is that at any point of decision, they may be more important than a particular instrumental tie. In the context of markets this may mean that people behave in a manner which looks irrational to an observer expecting instrumental behaviour. In the context of a hierarchical relationship within an organization the formal hierarchical relationship between supervisor and supervisee may be overruled by an expressive tie between the two.[11]

'Differential mode of association'[12] means that people have different orders and patterns of relationships. These are organized into a set of ranked categories of relationships[13] which for each individual is centred on them. Any individual will have relationships in which they are superior, inferior, and equal. This means that individuals have different obligations arising from a series of relationships but that each individual is at the centre of his/her own network of relationships. This implies that networks are discontinuous, are based on each individual, and are different for each person.

Since each individual will have their own network, personal networks may connect any two organizations, although they are formally connected by instrumental or market relationships. The networks do not have boundaries congruent with organizational boundaries. This implies that in some cases the *guanxi* connections may be more important than the instrumental links between two organizations. To an economic rationalist these connections may seem corrupt. Preferential treatment of insiders has always caused upset to outsiders. Raising economic rationality to the level of a moral stance provides an ethical justification for the outsiders' feeling of exclusion.

In *guanxi* relationships the ethical basis of decisions is traditionally the set of obligations which arise from the relationship rather than a set of universal principles which apply in any situation. There are therefore no general moral rules outside the specific relationships.[14] The implications of this are far-reaching in the operation of markets, especially where impartial treatment of suppliers or customers is an expectation of participants in a market who do not have *guanxi* connections. One view of this ethical question is that the expressive ties are part of an older set of moral rules which have to be swept away to allow market-based resource allocation.[15]

Given that each individual has a set of *guanxi* connections of various types and importance, an individual's sense of belonging may not fall into neat categories of 'family', 'neighbourhood', or 'employers'. Chinese people often use their native-place relationships to do business, through 'the projection of consanguinity into space'.[16] The strength of Chinese network relationships has produced an economic entity, which crosses boundaries of nations and companies.[17] On the other hand the workplace may take on characteristics of the family, giving support to 'insiders' which would not be merited by a straightforward employment relationship.

So, Chinese and other societies in which there are expressive ties do not necessarily consist of systematic organizations, but of webs of personal relationships, some of which are closer and more important than others. The metaphor is a stone in a pond, creating more and less important circles around an individual, as opposed to a haystack, the metaphor for the West, with people tied into individual bundles representing family, employer, or other organization which claims the individual's affiliation.

This implies, for example, that the boundary between the Western categories of 'public' and 'private' and 'state' may be inappropriate: 'Now we can see that the boundary between the public and the private spheres is relative—we may even say ambiguous.' People move from very close to the centre of their circle to further out, according to circumstances. 'In this pattern of oscillating but differential social circles, public and private are relative concepts' and 'Westerners regard the state as an organization surpassing all smaller groups . . . But in traditional China, the concept of public was the ambiguous *tianxia* (all under heaven), whereas the state was seen as the emperor's family . . . The state and the public are but additional circles that spread out like the waves from the splash of each person's social influence.'[18] While public–private and individual–state relationships have obviously changed between then and now, the definitional point remains: we cannot expect to find 'Western' relationships and organizational boundaries in societies in which expressive ties are differential and may be more significant than instrumental connections.

These expressive ties can coexist with (or even be overtaken by) instrumental ties. Without being either a 'modernization' theorist or its opposite a 'culturalist', it is fairly obvious that in societies in which there is a lot of profit being made, there is more to relationships than these expressive ties. Business values in China and Hong Kong are indeed distant from Confucian values. We cannot explain or predict any behaviour deductively from these relationships.[19] In each case, we need to look at the actual relationships, in their historical and social context.[20] It does mean, though, that we should not approach relationships and values as if there is a single ideal type of relationship, of behaviour based on market ethics and historically and geographically confined definitions of organizational types and their boundaries.

It is possible that relationships will have elements of both expressive and instrumental ties. A business relationship may be tempered by kinship. The networks of companies in South China, Hong Kong, and Taiwan are based both on profitable partnerships and broad kinship ties. The same can be true of the relationships between government and business: the province of birth of the business owner and the state employee can be a determinant of decision-making, while operating broadly within the rule of law, hierarchically regulated. A kinship relationship may be tempered by instrumentality.

How the connections are maintained

The discussion of expressive and instrumental ties showed that there are at least two types of connections between people which will determine how they behave towards each other. There is also a third category, that of the exercise of authority which comes from a source other than economic strength in a transaction or from some form of family loyalty. The following section asks how the links are maintained in practice.

'Family' or 'expressive'

The idea of a family tie applies to people with shared parents or grandparents but these sorts of ties can extend to a series of concentric circles around the individual. In rural society they may extend to everyone in the village and then to everyone in the spouse's village. In urban societies these types of ties may be created among people who went to the same school (the classmate tie), served in the same army unit (the comrade tie), attend the same church (the congregation tie), or belong to the same club or society which may be secret. Freemasons and triad societies may be included here as well as golf clubs. Some of the expectations generated by membership of the same family may even extend to the ties between people from the same province, county, or region.

Such ties are not fixed forever. They may be generated and reinforced and they may break down or diminish in strength. Shared experiences may be reinforced by further shared experiences. Regimental ties are reinforced by reunions and reminiscence. Club ties are reinforced by contact and by the performance of rituals. Locational ties are reinforced by ritual visits to the home place at special times of the year. Family ties of family members who live a long way away are reinforced by family gatherings on special or tragic occasions (weddings, funerals, and religious festivals).

Family ties can be broken down too. It is possible that long periods of physical absence may make family members treat the ties as less strong. Migration over long distances with little chance of reinforcing rituals may weaken ties (although there are ways of maintaining ties over distance). Another source of weakening of the family tie is the generation of alternative connections. People who physically leave their families make new contacts in the place they move to. An example is male migrants who maintain two wives, one in the place of origin and one in the place of migration. The second wife generates obligations which may be similar to those towards the first. Or people may create friendships, classmate, and other ties which become more important than the family ties. If an individual is also socially mobile, the new ties may reflect a movement from one class position to another, such as from peasant to urban proletarian or from urban proletarian to middle class. Family ties can also be weakened by a desire to make money. Family members may be tempted to ignore obligations if, for example, there is a chance of making money by cheating a family member. Inheritance can cause a breakdown of the family ties among siblings competing for inheritance.

At any moment therefore the family ties may be more or less strong. An individual may be in transition from obeying all family obligations to behaving in a completely instrumental and self-interested way as the forces causing a breakdown of the expressive ties become stronger than the forces reinforcing them.

Economic transactions

Market transactions between individuals may also take different forms. It is often said that contracts may be complete or incomplete: an incomplete contract is necessary where neither side can predict all the elements of the transaction and is possible where there is a high degree of 'trust' between the parties. The word 'trust' should be confined to those ties which rely on obligations generated outside the particular transaction. Expressive ties, as described above, reflect obligations which would persist even in a market-type transaction between two members of the same family or other expressive group.

Outside of family ties, individuals may develop a degree of reliance on each other. Williamson's[21] work on transaction costs and Sako's[22] work on contracts, for example, show that there are ways of making transactions which may be seen as having various degrees of obligation. In one extreme, all transactions take the form of complete contracts that are backed by recourse to arbitration or law in the case of failure to meet the contract on either side. At the other extreme, contracts may be incomplete and cooperation and compromise may achieve adjustments to the performance of the contract by either side. Sako calls the extremes 'adversarial' and 'obligational'.

Adversarial transactions may occur, in Williamson's framework, where there is no need to enter obligational contracts because switching costs are low, where one side of the bargain has more knowledge than the other, and where the transactions are short term. Sako argues that adversarial contracts may be inefficient even when these conditions apply and that market structure is not the main determinant of the nature of the transactions.

Parties may try to develop obligational relationships because incomplete contracts and mutual trust may produce better outcomes for both sides of a bargain in the long run. Mutually beneficial transactions are more likely to arise from a shared interest in the outcome of the whole transaction, rather than each side trying to gain short-term advantage.

Adversarial transactions can also arise if one side can see a large short-term pay-off from operating in self-interest to the detriment of the other party or if one side can use its extra power to gain advantage over the other side. An important factor in economic transactions is the relative power of the two parties. Trade among people with equal market power will be different from trade between a dominant and submissive partner. A large manufacturer may dominate individual component suppliers, keep prices low, and dictate terms and conditions. The general proposition is that instrumental relationships that contain no element of expressive ties do not necessarily produce an equal relationship between the parties. Replacing an expressive tie by an instrumental one or more generally moving from a society in which expressive relationships are the most important determinant of action to one in which markets predominate does not necessarily mean that transactions will be more fair or more equitable.

'Authority'

Family ties of obedience contain elements of authority. Outside the family there are other forms of authority. Armies and bureaucracies operate through formal authority with punishment as a resort for offenders. The rule of law may also be an expression of authority of the state over individuals.

Authority may be imposed with different degrees of acceptance. In a society where people feel that they have a say in the exercise of authority, individuals may willingly accept the rule of law and the authority of the state. In societies where people accept hierarchy as a 'natural' phenomenon people lower down the hierarchy may accept instructions.

Where the law is perceived as illegitimate, for example when people see the state as an instrument of a ruling élite pursuing its own interests, then authority will only be accepted if backed up by force.

Regime type is an expression of the mode of imposition of authority. Social democratic regimes gain authority through acceptance. Authoritarian regimes maintain authority through coercion. In some circumstances, authority connections are the only alternative to expressive and instrumental links. But, when there is a breakdown of a network of different kinds of ties, how the state or anyone else copes with that breakdown depends on the regime type that is in place. In the 1997 meltdown, the strength of the regimes in PRC and Singapore made the events there less disastrous than in the (weakened by elections, divisions, and competition for power) governments of Korea and Japan.

In the rest of the book, the three sorts of relationship, expressive, instrumental, or market and relationships based on authority or force will be seen to be in tension in the spheres of the economy, politics, and social welfare. In the rest of this chapter the idea of networks built on a mixture of expressive, instrumental, and power relationships is explored.

MIXED TIES AND NETWORKS

In any society all three types of ties are likely to be operating at the same time. Any individual is likely to have family ties, authority ties outside the family, and economic ties within both of those and outside them. A son may obey his father because he is his father, may be a junior partner in the family business, and also doing transactions with companies outside the family. A worker may have family connections that produce obligations, an employment relationship that is based on authority, and an economic relationship with a landlord that is purely instrumental. A family business will have different relationships within the family business, with customers and suppliers, and with the government of the countries in which it operates.

Each kind of tie may be dynamic and may at any point be in transition from one degree of trust, obligation, or reliance to another. One implication of this is that behaviour may be unpredictable: someone may expect the other party to a transaction to behave in a way that reflects a family-type tie and then be cheated. Or someone may be expected to behave in a purely instrumental way, for example by accepting the lowest prices bid from a stranger, and then behave according to family ties and accept a higher bid from a family member.

The same can happen in politics. For example Chinese Malays were expected always to support the Chinese party but in 1995 many voted for the BN coalition.[23] An expressive tie of consanguinity was replaced either by a new expressive tie or by an instrumental one. They may have voted that way because they now feel more nationally Malay than ethnically Chinese or they may have thought that the policies of the BN were advantageous.

So far we have discussed only dyadic ties. Networks consist of nodes and the connections between them. In Fei's scheme, each individual is at the centre of his or her own network with a variety of ties to a variety of other nodes. In this case, an individual can be a member of many other people's networks that are all centred on themselves.

Nodes may be more than individuals. A group with strong ties (which may be of any type) and frequent contact may form a node in a network. The firm is a set of strongly connected nodes and may itself become a node in a network. This is not necessarily the case for all economic entities. A group of traders, for example, may share some facilities but have stronger connections outside the group than inside it. A group of companies, on the other hand, may have such strong ties with each other that they constitute a node even though the parts of the node are under different ownership. So a *keiretsu*[24] in Japan may be a node consisting of relatively equal connections. A *chaebol* may be a node in the economy and a dominated network. Nodes may themselves be networks of connections. Connections between nodes may consist of different types of ties between individuals in each node as well as connections between one whole node and another.

Nodes may be defined as identifiable groups of connected nodes. In this case, the relevant boundary may not be the formal or legal organizations. If there are closer connections among, say members of a political party and civil servants in a ministry through some form of family tie (whether classmate, genetic, or whatever), then it makes sense to treat the network as the unit of analysis, rather than the party or the ministry.

One type of network has no dominating member and people work collaboratively, according to mutual self-interest rather than expressive ties. These are essentially markets with many participants. There may be regulation in the markets or laws which affect transactions, but the relationships are essentially based on transactions which each side hopes will bring them benefits.

Other networks have a dominating member and behave more like hierarchies than networks that are not dominated by one node; the mutuality is distorted by the fact that some members are more dependent than others. As Castells[25] says, the networks of companies surrounding the *chaebol* in Korea are an example of a hierarchical network.

However, just as dyadic relationships can be based on a mixture of expressive and instrumental ties, so can networks. Even in a network state, there can be competition among networks, conflict between families and nonproductive (in the sense of 'national development') pursuit of power. As Moon and Prasad[26] say: ' This does not imply that all these relationships are harmonious: East Asian states are not necessarily unitary actors, and networks between the state and society are, more often than not, governed by the politics of conflict, disharmony and friction.'

Networks and classes

Classes create networks: the KMT created networks of clients among the old, displaced landowners and among the emerging Taiwanese small- and medium-business class. As well as licences and contracts from the KMT, votes and support went the other way. Such networks may become unsustainable if they rely entirely on economic ties and do not generate 'family'-type obligations that would persist even if there were not enough money to keep paying for loyalty. The recent election results in Taiwan show that these relationships probably did not develop into anything more than a purely economic tie operated in an instrumental way.

As fractions of classes grow (for example an emerging trading class or a professional class) the dominant class will try to include them in their networks. They can do this by inviting them to join the places where network connections are made, by making sure their children go to the same schools, or by inviting them to stand for political office for the same party.

When networks get too big to incorporate all the growing classes (because there is no room or time for contact or because the interests may conflict too much for the new classes to be incorporated), then new powerful nodes may develop. Eventually these nodes may come to dominate the network. Sometimes classes are networks. If there is a 'finance capital' class, it exists as a network of connections among individuals and the institutions they control.

Classes may create networks by making many kinds of connections: family, money transactions, fear and/or terror, exploitation. For example the Mafia was created through families, by control of the scarce water supply (wells in Sicily), through terrorizing those who refused to pay. Not every node in a network has equal power.

Sometimes networks are classes. The ruling class in pre-industrial Europe was a network of family connections joined by intermarriages designed to maximize landownership. Landlord classes make family connections in this way in most agricultural societies.

The diversity of the connections between nodes and a social network and the variety of expressive, instrumental, and power ties mean that 'network' is not a simple category, nor does it have much explanatory power on its own. To speak of a society being a 'network society' is a simplification of this complexity. To understand the networks, the nature of the connections must be made explicit. In what follows, what defines the dominant way in which a society is governed is not the presence or absence of networks but the nature of the connections. If a society is governed mainly by expressive ties, it can be said that its governance is based on connections, rather than instrumental relationships such as market relationships. Societies may also have networks that consist of instrumental relationships and these can also form networks of connections among businesses and between spheres such as politics and business.

Networks and states

Networks cross borders, sometimes making the network more important than the nation or state. MNCs have networks of economic transactions among companies and sometimes national politicians. Trans-border economic networks may be more powerful than within-border family, authority, or economic ties.

International organizations such as the World Bank, the IMF, and the Asian Development Bank have members with ideological connections on policy and personal connections within states, which may produce policy decisions which are different from those which would have been reached by the national governments operating without those connections. There may be at times also authority relations: the IMF rescue of Korea allowed policies to be imposed on the national government.

Networks within nations can be more important than state–society relationships. If there are strong family-type networks in a nation, they may be more important entities than the institutions. For example, family-type connections between trade unions and government may be stronger than authority-type relationships through which trade union members control their leaders. Or family-type networks between leading members of companies and politicians in governments may be more important than authority ties between civil servants and those same companies

Classes can set up networks in their own interests by going beyond their immediate connections and incorporating other important groups. Ties consisting of client-type relationships that are essentially economic and may generate long-term obligations can be used to ensure that new nodes do not form but that existing nodes remain within a dominated network (Taiwan, Malaysia).

Network breakdown

If the class loses control to another class, its networks may degenerate. Other ties offering better returns may supersede networks of obligations that are essentially economic transactions. If a party in government is outbid for support by another, richer party, it may lose control of the government. In periods of industrialization, parties which only have networks among landowners and farmers may lose to parties whose networks consist of increasingly rich capitalists. The same may happen when the financial sector becomes more important that the industrial.

As economies develop, the old ruling élites may find it difficult to incorporate all the new classes and fractions in their network. Apart from the creation of networks by essentially economic ties and clientilism, networks based on family or geography may become less powerful as people from different family networks gain economic power. So, the Shanghainese who dominated Hong Kong had to give away some power to people from other provinces. In the 1997 elections in Taiwan the mainland KMT gave way in part to indigenous Taiwanese.

Networks can also break down because of instability caused by incompatible ties, faced with an external shock. Take a hypothetical example: a Ministry of Finance has an authority tie over a bank and instructs the bank to make a loan to a conglomerate. The authority is backed by a willingness to underwrite the loan with public funds, backed by borrowing from foreigners. At the same time, there are family connections between the Ministry and the conglomerate: brothers occupy positions in both and they have mutual obligations that are expressive. Meanwhile, the conglomerate makes a borrowing arrangement with the bank that is outside normal practice (lower cover and lower interest than is warranted by the risk, because the risk is shared by the taxpayer). If the bank then has liquidity problems because of bad debts, it may be forced to call in the loan for 'normal' market or commercial reasons. This is not a problem if the underwriting Ministry of Finance has the funds to cover the debt. If the Ministry of Finance has entered many such agreements, at some point it will run out of cash. If it has borrowed from other lenders to enable it to back loans, its relationship with those lenders will also be affected by the call on funds.

At one level the collapse of this unstable three-node network can be explained as a simple case of gearing being too high and banks being over-stretched. But the obvious question follows: how did the borrowers and lenders get into this position in the first place? The answer could take several forms at different levels. The obvious answer is 'because they could'. When there were many profitable projects and sales were growing, the lending was in any case relatively low risk. The expressive connections simply shifted loans from slightly less risky to slightly more risky projects. At another level, the case arises because there were connections involved which were not guided by commercial principles at all, in the sense of decisions being made purely on the basis of an economic calculus for each individual. The financial (economic) outcome, which the parties sought, was joint and several optimization, rather than individual optimization. In other words, a network based on expressive ties tried to maximize its returns.

The collapse can similarly be explained at different levels: falling profitability leads to inability to meet loan obligations. The number of cases outstripped the Ministry of Finance's capacity to guarantee loans, so the financial system collapsed. At another level we could say that the economic reality of the instrumental ties, especially of the foreign lenders who were outside the expressive network, conflicted with and eventually replaced the expressive ties.

IMPLICATIONS

The intervention by the IMF can be understood as part of an effort by institutions and companies outside the region to shift the balance of modes of governance from an emphasis on expressive connections towards greater emphasis on instrumental economic ties, or from rule by connections to rule by the market. It was not concerned with the degree to which the countries involved were ruled by powerful élites unless they were operating through expressive connections. Criticism or calls for change in regime type is not part of the brief of the IMF, rather it is concerned with establishing liberal market economies.

In what follows it will be seen that in the spheres of the economy, politics, the family, and the civil service there is a variety of balance between rule by connections, by market, and by the exercise of power. In some cases there can be seen a clear tendency dating from before the crisis to move towards rule by market and a tendency to reduce authoritarianism. The crisis has accelerated the move towards the market especially in Korea and Japan. Does this imply that the region is converging on a single model of governance that rejects the culturally based way of operating through family and other expressive connections and that it will soon join a global model of rule by markets operating according to the same rules and ethics? There are people who take this view, including Kim Dae Jung the President of Korea. The forces of the global market are leading to more openness to foreign trade and investment and to a homogenization of business and government practices. An alternative view is that nations can maintain their own practices and cultural differences if they participate in a minimal set of common standards. Just as the international institutions have tolerated regime types from dictatorships to kleptocracies to democracies, so they can tolerate differences in modes of governance. For example, the PRC's application to join the WTO will be decided by its trading rules not by its party-state apparatus or its practice of connection-based governance.

NOTES

1. E. W. Said, *Orientalism* (London: Routledge & Kegan Paul, 1978).
2. See W. W. Bevis, *Borneo Log* (Seattle and London: Washington University Press, 1995).
3. *Far East Economic Review*, 17 July 1998: 12.
4. Moon Chung-in and R. Prasad, 'Beyond the Developmental State: Networks, Politics, and Institutions', *Governance*, 7/4 (1994): 373.
5. e.g. J. Tao and G. Drover, 'Chinese and Western Notions of Need', *Critical Social Policy*, 49/16 (1996) and J. Tao, 'The Moral Foundation of Welfare in Chinese Society: Between Virtues and Rights', in G. K. Becker (ed.), *Ethics in Business and Society* (Berlin: Springer, 1996).
6. The term 'economic rationalism' has been used in Australia to encompass all policies of the coalition government that deny any obligations or rights outside the free market.
7. A. Y. So and S. W. K. Chiu, *East Asia and the World Economy* (London: Sage, 1995): 9.
8. See F. Fukuyama, *Trust* (New York: Free Press, 1995).
9. See M. Sako, *Prices, Quality and Trust* (Cambridge: Cambridge University Press, 1992) and K. Jones, 'Trust as an Affective Attitude', *Ethics*, 107/Oct. (1996): 4–25.
10. See Fei Xiatong, *From the Soil (Xiangtu Zhongguo)*, trans. G. Hamilton and W. Zheng (Berkeley and Los Angeles: University of California Press, 1948, 1992).
11. e.g. to cope with this possibility, the Hong Kong civil service has a rule that if a family member is posted to a section where there is a junior member of the family, the junior is automatically posted elsewhere.
12. *Chaxugeju.*
13. *Shehui guanxi.*

14. Among other things, this has profound implications for the notion of 'rights' which are situation-specific, rather than universal— see J. Tao, 'The Moral Foundation of Welfare'.

15. After all, Aristotle spoke of the difference between people dealing with each other in a traditional way and in the market. Weber wrote about *gessellschaft* and *gemeinschaft*, Ouchi applied the idea of 'market, hierarchies and clans' to the study of societies and organizations. W. G. Ouchi, 'Markets, bureaucracies and clans', in G. Thompson (ed.), *Markets, Hierarchies and Networks: The Coordination of Social Life* (London: Sage, 1991).

16. Fei Xiatong, *From the Soil*: 123.

17. See M. Weidenbaum and S. Hughes, *The Bamboo Network: How Expatriate Chinese are Creating a New Economic Superpower in Asia* (New York: Martin Kessler Books, 1996).

18. Fei Xiatong, *From the Soil*: 69–7.

19. Any more than you can predict behaviour deductively from rules of utility maximization, unless, of course, you are an economist.

20. This is fairly obvious and not much different from Jessop: 'rather than trying to define the core of the state in *a priori* terms, we need to explore how its boundaries are established through specific practices within and outside the state'. B. Jessop, *State Theory* (Pennsylvania: Pennsylvania University Press, 1990): 366.

21. O. Williamson, *Markets and Hierarchies* (NewYork: The Free Press, 1975).

22. M. Sako, *Prices, Quality and Trust*.

23. See E. T. Gomez, *The 1995 Malaysian General Elections* (Singapore: Institute of Southeast Asian Studies, 1996): occasional paper 93.

24. A '*keiretsu*' is a group of companies trading with each other frequently.

25. M. Castells, *The Rise of the Network Society* (Oxford: Blackwell, 1996).

26. Moon Chung-in and R. Prasad, 'Beyond the Developmental State': 376–7.

3

The Economy and the State

INTERVENTION AND THE MARKET

There has been a debate about the implications for policy for economic development elsewhere of the Asian economic success whose extremes could be described as liberal, emphasizing the merits of markets and 'statist', emphasizing the merits of planning and government intervention. While neither side would probably accept such a crude dichotomy, there were two camps. On the one hand, the liberals believed that all decisions about capital allocation or lending should left to the market. All interference by governments through import restrictions, foreign investment controls, pricing, tariffs, and differential taxation would always produce an allocation of resources less favourable than if those decisions were left to the market. 'Favourable' is defined as producing high growth rates.

The opposite position has many variants. One says that the 'market' generates unequal development, that there is a metropolitan 'core' in the world economy, and that the rest of the world will inevitably be used by businesses in that core as a source of cheap materials and cheap labour. Only intervention by governments in the periphery to resist the results of the market forces will save those countries from having permanently second-class economies and incomes. A variant is that there are sub-cores, which may develop their own sub-peripheries. Either way, there were three decades of better than world average growth in Japan and Korea and both experiences included active ministries, economic planning, directed credit, a deliberate effort to create industries where none existed, selective control on imports, and support for exports. These two cases showed, say the proponents of this line, that governments could beat the market and could help create economies which are richer and grow faster than would be the case if such things were left purely to business and the market.

The economic collapse provided sustenance to both camps. The liberals could argue that the credit crises in Korea and Japan were a result of overprotection of lenders by governments. When governments were unable to honour their underwriting of loans, the loans were called in, banks failed, and companies went bankrupt. 'I told you so' was heard, showing that after all banks and investors left both undirected and unprotected make better decisions in the long run than governments.

The 'statists' could argue the opposite. The long period of growth in Korea, the thirty-plus years of growth in Japan until the recession and in Taiwan, and the sudden spurts of growth in Malaysia, Indonesia, and to some extent Thailand had all been guided in part by governments and ministries of industry and finance. Underwriting of loans, whether tacit or explicit, made growth faster by mobilizing capital more quickly. The crisis, far from being the result of too much government and too much regulation, was the result of speculation and too much exposure to the market. Greedy lenders overstretched themselves, underestimated risks, and overestimated returns. When risks became apparent they panicked and overreacted, dropping stocks, calling in loans, and getting out of currencies to an extent that was not called for by the underlying economic performance of the national economies which were left to suffer currency devaluations, stock and property market collapses, and rising unemployment. Previously orderly allocations of resources, overseen by government agencies, were replaced by wild swings in prices and movements of cash.

THE 'DEVELOPMENTAL STATE'

The developmental state argument, made by Chalmers Johnson and others, was that the connection between the state and business was not simply one of 'interference' or 'direction' by the state of the market. It was rather a positive partnership involving many connections between entities such as MITI in Japan and the major industrial players. The Japanese economy is the origin of the expression 'developmental state',[1] with its combination of state banks, economic planning and steering, an alliance between finance, government, and business, and pursuit of an ideology of national development. He points to the appointment of retired civil servants to jobs in industry as an example of the interlocking of government and business in Japan:

it is sometimes supposed that government and business are two distinct entities and that the close co-operation between them reflects a pervasive 'consensus' in Japanese society. This view overlooks the fact that in many critical industries the businessmen who have dealings with government officials are themselves retired government officials, and that in industries where there are large numbers of retired bureaucrats . . . there is much more 'government-business-consensus' than in industries where such relations do not exist.[2]

In any case, the argument did not apply to the whole region, the connections between business and government having been especially strong in

Japan and Korea. For example, Macintyre argues that the developmental state idea only applied to north-east Asia and that rapid growth occurred in 'Thailand, Malaysia and Indonesia, with states that appear markedly weaker (but) have also managed to achieve impressive results'.[3] In other words, the 'developmental state' notion was restricted geographically and was not a necessary condition for fast economic growth.

'GOOD GOVERNANCE'

The 'good governance' approach takes a normative view of the relationships, arguing for more clarity in the distinctions between institutions. A good example is Hilton Root[4] who wrote a book commissioned by the Asia Development Bank to interpret the importance of good governance to economic growth. In an appendix called 'Institution Building for Development', Root sets out the rules of good governance which include accountability, transparency, and predictability. The rest of the list is concerned with institutional capacity building, including the civil service, local government, and 'civil society'. Only countries which practise good governance will grow: 'The globalization of world capital markets will benefit those countries that practice good governance.'[5]

This approach is based on two assumptions about the relationship between business and government. First, government and civil service can be disconnected from business by all ties other than official ones. Second, technocratic state employees can identify 'national interest' or 'development' and pursue them impartially. By doing so they can defeat 'rent-seeking' behaviour by people who want to get rich without playing the free-market game, and by doing so produce suboptimal economic outcomes.

The difference between the 'developmental state' and the 'good governance' approaches is that the developmental state argument is essentially about the interconnectedness of the government and business spheres. The good governance approach is about creating institutional arrangements that break down that interconnectedness and establish more instrumental relationships between the two.

Kuo's interpretation of the 'developmental state' argument is that it mistakenly treats the state as isolated: 'What is wrong with the developmental state theory is its tendency to treat the state as a "closed system" aloof from its social environment . . . The state, business associations, firms and other economic actors have to be studied from the perspective of "open systems".'[6] This statement captures more of the complexity of the relationships than a description that makes a very sharp divide between business and government and is very close to Chalmers Johnson's position which is that the developmental state consists of a close set of connections between the spheres of government, finance, and industry.

THE DEVELOPMENT OF THE DEBATE

Robert Wade[7] set out the development of the argument between the 'developmental state' camp and the neoclassical or liberal economists. The neoclassical camp argued that the success, especially of Japan and Korea, would have been even greater if the state had been less involved in economic development, especially directing credit towards particular industries. Permanent protection or credit subsidy distorted resource allocation away from optimality. Since resources were allocated by administrative mechanisms, bureaucrats would be inclined to take bribes or other inducements rather than allocate them according to economic criteria. An argument developed that in all cases the free market was better than 'interference'.

Wade[8] has also chronicled the IMF's determination to resist Japan's interpretation of the relationship between the state and economic growth and to defend the United States' version. The IMF, staffed mainly by US and British trained economists and strong advocates of the free-market line, found themselves challenged by another interpretation of history from Japan which, incidentally, was becoming an important IMF contributor. Each side had reasons to defend its position, in addition to their contestation for the ownership of the truth. The IMF had to denigrate the wisdom of officials, however expert, getting involved in the details of economic decision-making. This was not only an ideological commitment but a self-interested one. IMF officials, promoting their universal, homogeneous solutions to particular heterogeneous problems could not admit that detailed knowledge by bankers of the real world of particular economies was of any importance for economic success. Ministry of Finance officials in Japan had precisely the opposite interest. While Japan was booming the role of the intelligent, well-informed but disinterested public official, whether in the Ministry of Finance or MITI was proclaimed as key. Coordination, direction of credit, selective use of import controls, arrangement of incentives were all claimed as essential ingredients in Japan's success. The officials who thought that they represented these virtues naturally wanted to claim success.

Neither extreme position represented the complexity of the actual relationships between government and industry. MITI was not disinterested and spent a lot of effort to recruit and incorporate industry representatives, for example in the telecom industries into the Ministry and to represent the interest of Japanese firms in international negotiations. Nor has there been a free market, in the liberals' sense, in many industries in many countries. From arms and aerospace to property development and agriculture, governments have had an interest in and an influence over one or other of investment, pricing, and location decisions, whether through procurement policy, zoning, licensing, tariffs or price controls. The extreme liberal position represents at best a few industries in a few countries for short periods.

If the liberals accepted the idea of a developmental state, it was only as a stage of economic development. After all, Europe had gone through its period of state-led reconstruction, financed in part by lend-lease and Marshall Plan aid. Eventually, nationalized industries had been privatized and state licensing and controls had been eased as markets developed. Perhaps the Japanese and Korean states had been both strong and engaged in directive planning and interventions, but they, like Europe before them, would eventually replace the state with the market. Market failure would eventually be replaced by state failure and in turn replaced by the market. The point was that in the long run the market is best. The 'good governance' argument is that by states doing only what is necessary because of market failure and more lately because of the effects of inequality, and by doing it in a transparent and disinterested manner, states can promote economic development through prudence, honesty, and frugality.

The World Bank made a very slight move away from the liberal camp. Its *World Development Report* for 1997 was advertised as marking a change in the bank's attitude towards the state, recognizing that states do essential things and can do them well. The summary of the report said: 'An effective state is vital for the provision of goods and services—and the rules and institutions— that allow markets to flourish and people to lead healthier, happier lives.'[9] It seemed as if US anti-state dominance of World Bank thinking about the state was over. But the framework for thinking about the state put forward in the full report[10] was still based on 'market failure'—the idea that the 'state' should 'intervene' only where markets fail to produce a good or service—and of a need to improve equity in the distribution of benefits in society. It warned of the dangers of 'state bureaucracies being granted too much. When that happens, state officials at all levels may pursue their own agendas rather than society's.'[11] The only example of officials using the state for their own personal gain that they quote is Haiti under the Duvaliers.

NETWORKS AND ECONOMIC DEVELOPMENT

At the extreme, it could be that the state and business sectors are so open to each other that the two categories are not the most relevant to describe the situation. If families or élite groups control countries through a network of institutional connections, then the connections are the relevant category for analysis. This is so obvious in the PRC where party and factional connections control different parts of the economy that the categories 'state' and 'business' clearly do not apply to the SOE sector, nor to the TVE sector at local level. Rachel Murphy found that in Taiyuan, Shanxi Province, the connections between the private sector entrepreneurs and state (province) organizations were not so much official ones as personal connections with individual public servants: 'Instead of organizing and seeking concessions from the state, entrepreneurs purchase favour from the relevant department or official in an individual capacity.'[12]

Not only are there not legally based and predictable relationships between enterprises and the state. Murphy suggests that 'the vulnerability of entrepreneurs has promoted the interpenetration of state and society because the interest maximising strategies employed by private entrepreneurs share the common rationale of functioning in an individual capacity to secure ties with the state machine.'[13]

There is a middle position, between the neoclassical and the 'developmental state' lines. Gary Hamilton[14] has argued that Taiwan's period of rapid growth was not primarily driven by the state. The state enterprises were mainly in 'upstream' products, such as steel and energy, which responded to the growth of the rest of the economy rather than created it. Most of the export-led growth came from the manufacturing sector, made up of small and medium-sized family-owned businesses. Many of the attempts by the state and its planners to direct the economy have failed: the attempt to create large trading companies, integrated contracting networks, an export-oriented transport industry, and state credit for small and medium-sized businesses all failed. He argues instead that Taiwan's economy has special characteristics, based on horizontal *guanxi* linkages and vertical control of firms by families. Government simply has to accept that this is how the economy is structured and managed and work within that framework.

Wade has argued for the 'governed market' approach, that governments have been successful in governing markets, rather than controlling them. He argues that governments cannot create industries or whole sectors where there is not the capacity in the private sector nor the opportunity in the market for such industries. Indeed there are cases of failed government attempts to create industries or sectors in the most rapidly growing economies.

Wade, Kuo, and Hamilton all go beyond the caricature arguments based on the assumption that there are two distinct categories, the 'state' and the 'economy'. The idea that states 'intervene' in economies to a greater or lesser extent is based on the history of the development of the state in Europe, rather than the development of post-war countries in Asia. Only in the case of Taiwan, in which the 'state' was imported in the persons of the KMT from the mainland, can there said to have been a clear division between 'state' and 'society'. In the process of nation-building, the élites used a variety of institutional forms, including ministries, the army, banks, and businesses. The forms of ownership also varied, from individual to state ownership and included ownership of businesses by the party, the KMT.

We saw in the previous Section that the stark distinction between the 'developmental state' school and the free marketeers is not as absolute as it might appear, at least on the developmental state side. None of those commentators claimed that there was no role for the market or that Japan and Korea were run as command economies. More importantly, nobody claims that developmental states have not made mistakes, backed the wrong industries or the wrong companies, wasted money, and made less than perfect decisions. In this Section the argument is that élites in different countries in the region have used different instruments to develop the economies, to make money, and gain or retain power for themselves. Sometimes the instrument has been the state, using a variety of measures, such as direct investment, directed credit, licences, and permissions. On other occasions companies and banks have been created, sometimes in 'networks' of connections in which companies lend to or invest in each other, sometimes with state backing in a way which is very different from a 'free market' in capital or services.

On some occasions, the distinction between the state and the party is very hard to see, especially in Taiwan and the PRC. In other cases, the distinction between the state and the ruling family or families is hard to see, as in Indonesia under the Suharto ruling family, or the Philippines under the Marcoses. And certainly the very close connections between ministries, banks, and companies in Japan and Korea, especially as revealed by the various bankruptcies and crises, make the idea of there being an independent, technocratic bureaucracy devoted to economic rationality and the national good rather hard to believe.

The other argument is about whether these network-type relationships are (or were before the crisis) in a process of breaking down to be replaced by more instrumental market relationships. Did the denationalizations, for example, constitute a replacement of hierarchical and expressive relationships by a more anonymous and impartial set of market relationships? Under market rule firms can go bankrupt, workers sell their labour for money rather than establishing a lifelong set of rights and obligations with a state employer, and investments and loans are made on the basis of a rational appraisal of economic prospects rather than political and family connections.

In Taiwan, the state was a major instrument for the development of the economy. The nationalist government took over the companies owned by the Japanese *zaibatsu*[15] and the Japanese government at the end of the Second World War, which accounted for over half of GDP in the 1950s. While some have been privatized, there remain state-owned enterprises in strategic sectors which still accounted for around 18 per cent of GDP (in 1992). In addition the ruling party, the KMT,[16] also owns about 150 companies and has assets of about US$3 billion.[17] Since the KMT has lost its monopoly on political power, there has been more disclosure of its holdings and business practices. In 1993 a law[18] was passed which required some openness. As a result the KMT disclosed that it had seven holding companies. Until the 1980s many of the KMT's companies had been monopolies. For example, Chung Hsing Bills Finance Co. was one of only three companies allowed to operate bills financing, Fu Hwa Securities Finance Co. had exclusive rights in margin trading and selling stock on credit, and the party owned the ten companies which distributed natural gas.

1993 was also the year in which the fourteenth National Party Congress decided to change the way it used its investments. Until the formation of the DPP, the KMT and the state were indistinguishable, as were party and state funds. It was difficult to see which funds belonged to which entity and funds could be made available for industries or projects as the leadership chose. When the party disentangled its finances from that of the state, it started expanding its holdings. From 1988 to 1993 the party opened a new enterprise on average every two months. The change in 1993 was that profit, rather than influence, became the main objective. The party formed a Business Management Committee, which was to be chaired by Liu Tai-ying, a former classmate of Lee Teng-hui and a well-connected person.

The party divested itself of companies which generated criticism—it sold four of its gas companies and reduced its shareholdings in many other companies. It listed some of its companies on the Taiwan Stock Exchange and reduced its holdings in these listed companies to less than 50 per cent. As well as diverting criticism, these listings also turned out to be very profitable. In 1997 it 'donated' its shares in the Central News Agency to the central government.

This relationship between the party and the economy also extends to close ties between the KMT and privately owned businesses. When the land reform was carried out, the landowning families were partly compensated with shares in state-owned enterprises, some of which ended up under the families' control. So, while there has been a programme of 'denationalization', the state and the party still own and control significant businesses and the transfer of ownership has not necessarily changed the locus of control to a different set of interests. The current privatization programme includes 104 companies with net assets of about US$650 billion but excludes the companies owned by the KMT. It is too early to see who is buying the industries as they are denationalized. If it is the case that they are bought by KMT or closely related entities, the transfer of ownership will be of symbolic significance only. Opposition politicians argue that even minority holdings give the party a great deal of influence: new party member of the legislature Fu Kuen-chen said: 'the KMT may control only 18 per cent of shares but that 18 per cent is crucial because it provides easy access to government'.[19]

Kuo[20] shows that the state and the business associations in Taiwan always worked closely together, rather than the state being a separate entity. The business associations were developed by the state to have a mode of control outside government and market. They also prevented or hindered the development of genuinely independent business associations.

These were the main methods in which the KMT influenced the business sector: ownership of businesses and industries, either through the government or the party; share ownership of other businesses; and control or influence of business associations. It also used credit, especially while it was trying to develop export industries, through subsidized loans and special loan funds.

None of these methods allowed complete party domination of business although of course they allowed a lot of influence. Towards the end of 1998 the Korean government was promoting the virtues of the Taiwan way of relating government to business as opposed to the Korean way. It is clear from this short account that the Korean spokespeople overestimate the degree of liberalism and the lack of interference of the state and the party in business in Taiwan.

In PRC, there has also been some denationalization of state-owned enterprises (SOEs) and township and village enterprises (TVEs), which is sometimes characterized as indicating China's transition to a capitalist, market-based economy. The state-owned enterprise sector became an increasing burden on government spending as the sector as a whole became less profitable. By 1995, the cost of subsidies has been estimated at $US 50 billion or 50 per cent of state spending.[21] Similarly, as competition intensified, some townships and villages sold their less profitable TVEs to their managers.

However, there are two reasons to be cautious about interpreting these two tendencies as part of the withdrawal of the 'state' from the 'economy'. The first is that the TVEs were not a standard form of state ownership, as known in the West. Many were officially owned by the local people of the township or village, controlled by local officials[22] but the workers are often peasants from the countryside or from other provinces, often employed at low wages and without the benefits of urban registration or membership of an urban work unit (education, housing, healthcare, pensions, sick pay). The profits from such enterprises were distributed among their founders.[23] Some TVEs became very successful. For example, one village in Shandong province now owns the Cockatoo Inn in Los Angeles.[24]

The second reason is that the meaning of public and private ownership is not very clear. For example, the People's Liberation Army has become a significant trading company since it was made a profit centre. How should this be classified—as part of the global trend towards privatization, or as a set of activities and relationships with Chinese characteristics and unlike anything that is happening in other economies. The strict distinction between what is publicly owned and what is privately owned does not apply in the case of the TVEs. Often the manager who has been working under contract is allowed to purchase part of the future profit stream as an alternative to a salary. The assets and land rights might remain with the original owners. Even if the asset is transferred to a new owner, investment decisions may remain with the local party through control over development and possibly credit.

The third reason is the great reluctance to privatize too many SOEs for fear of the political consequences. There is already significant unemployment which has been caused by the failure of SOEs which are still technically in existence, especially in the north-west, but can no longer pay their staff.[25] The consequences are especially harsh, since the enterprises were responsible for almost all aspects of the welfare of their workers as well as for paying their wages. Too widespread closures could lead to unrest and other consequences. Until a solution can be found to the problem of what happens to the displaced workers when enterprises are made profitable or closed down, we should not expect large-scale denationalization. Having said that, the state-owned sector is declining as a proportion of GDP as the other sectors grow.

The most significant privatization of production, of course, was the agricultural reform which replaced collective agriculture with the Household Responsibility System. There is no doubt that this was a significant switch in social relationships in the countryside, whatever the technicalities of the landownership system.

In Hong Kong, the booming service industries are almost entirely free from government interference, apart from normal stock-market regulation and so on. The government's actions to prop up the stock market in 1998 was out of character. However, in manufacturing there is a slightly different trend. Manufacturing employment in Hong Kong is now around 300,000, while it is estimated that the 30,000 Hong Kong companies operating in Guandong province employ about 5 million people.[26] These enterprises operate under the Chinese regime, with all that that implies in terms of local government regulation, whatever payments have to be made in order to stay in business, and local law. The connections between the Hong Kong owners and the local officials are an important part of the way those businesses operate. In other words, one aspect of Hong Kong's economy, the manufacturing hinterland, was part of the Chinese political economy long before the restoration of Chinese sovereignty.

Malaysia was, in some sense, a planned economy, having published its latest ten-year plan in 1996. The industrial development of Malaysia has been led by the government since Mahatir Mohammed started the 'Look East Policy'[27] which was designed to follow what he saw as Japan and Korea's growth path with basic industries supported by the state as an early investment for growth. The current plan emphasizes high-technology industries and a reduction in investment in labour-intensive industries that are causing a labour shortage.[28] The development of a 'Multi Media Super Corridor', including a big investment by Microsoft is an example of the way the Malaysian government promotes development. There are also close family ties between government and business.

Korea appeared as a paradox: it has had fast economic growth but is famous for bureaucratic sloth and corruption. As the *Washington Post* put it: 'the old system intertwined private money with government power to create one of the twentieth-century's truly miraculous sprints of economic growth. And no one here is quite sure that a bribe-free system will perform so well.'[29]

The connections between the military regime and the growing *chaebol* were closer than mere bribery, rather a set of networks which between them ran the country. Whether 'convergence' is occurring in Korea, defined as a clearer separation between state and business and a reduction in the role of the state, depends on whether these networks have been broken up by the recent bribery trials. The detention of two ex-presidents, nine *chaebol* heads, numerous ministers, and various relatives of the current government may indicate that the old system is being dismantled, or may be part of an internal power struggle to control the old system. This is certainly what President Kim Dae Jung thought when he was a prominent dissident (see Box 3.1).

There remains in Korea a significant state-owned and managed industrial and banking sector[30] which were part of the state-sponsored growth. There remain in place tariff and other protections for Korean industry, including a ban on consumer goods imports from Japan.

Box 3.1 Anti-Corruption Campaign in Korea

President Kim Young Sam started an anti-corruption campaign soon after he was elected in 1993. He stopped the practice of people being allowed to hide money and property under false names and forced public figures to declare their assets. He targeted even his own Minister of Defence, who was accused of taking bribes in relation to a helicopter project, and the wife of the Minister of Health.

The opposition, including future President Kim Dae Jung, accused the president of selecting only his enemies for prosecution. Chung Ju Yung, chairman of Hyundai who ran against Kim in the 1992 election and Park Chul On, a challenger for the party leadership, were prosecuted on tax evasion and corruption charges. In contrast, Lee Won Jo who was believed to be responsible for raising funds for the ruling party's candidates was convicted on corruption charges but received a suspended sentence.

Whether selective or not, the heads of most of the major *chaebol* were convicted of corruption, including Daewoo, Dong Ah, Jinro, Hanbo, Samsung, Daelim, Daeho Construction, Dongbu Group. Many received suspended sentences and others were released early.

In addition, two former presidents, Chun Doo-hwan and Roh Tae Woo were convicted and jailed for corruption, mutiny and treason in relation to the 1979 coup and the subsequent Kangjiu massacre. Initially Chun had received a death sentence. Just before Christmas 1997 they were both released from jail. Their release was agreed between Kim Dae Jung and Kim Young Sam, the outgoing president. Kim Dae Jung had himself been sentenced to death by the military regime for his part in inciting the riots that resulted in the Kwangjiu massacre but his sentence was commuted and he was released after two years in jail. Both former presidents attended Kim Dae Jung's inauguration ceremony.

If the state does withdraw from the economic intervention that built Korea's economy, it will be because forces outside the government-military-*chaebol* networks challenge that hegemony. The Hanbo and Sammi affairs (see Box 3.2) showed that the close relationship between finance, government, and production was not healthy for any of the parties in the long run. In a sense this affair epitomizes the problems caused by companies built with very high gearing based on loans made for reasons other than 'normal' financial criteria. This problem did not happen in Japan's period of rapid growth, partly because finance was available from its colonial empire and partly because loans were more tightly controlled.

The collapse of Yamaichi showed that until very recently, the Japanese government had been very willing to support ailing businesses (see Box 3.3).

Indonesia under the Sukarno and Suharto regimes was a different case. An

Box 3.2 Hanbo and Sammi

In January 1997 Hanbo Steel Industry Co. collapsed. It had received $6 billion in government loans, for which it offered collateral of $105 million. When Sammi also declared bankruptcy two months later, the government declared that it would no longer bail out companies that made losses. The Minister of Finance and Economy, Kang Kyung Shik told a news conference: 'the government no longer could and would rescue poorly managed bankrupt companies with taxpayers' money . . . In the past, the government has used the domestic banks as the conduit of "policy loans", to help finance strategic industries and preventing large conglomerates, particularly thirty leading ones, from going bankrupt. This means that the *chaebol* only had to become "too big to fail" with every way and means available.' This was a major policy change: the history of the *chaebol* had been one of close connections between the banks, the state, and the companies. Loans were all in practice guaranteed by the government. One of the reasons for the financial collapse was the government's stated intention of ending this practice.

Sammi Business Group, which included five subsidiary companies bought 100 per cent of two North American companies in 1989, Atlas Corp in Canada and Al-Tech Corp in the USA. Its overseas acquisitions made losses and its home plants suffered from the worldwide slump in steel demand. Sammi borrowed to cover the losses: by the end of 1996 its debts amounted to 1,899 billion won, of which Sammi Steel owed 1,241 billion. According to the published accounts, Sammi Steel had been making consistent losses: 79bn. in 1992, 89bn. in 1993, 68bn. in 1994, 39bn. in 1995 and 120bn. in 1996. In September 1997 Jinro, South Korea's largest liquor manufacturer, also went bankrupt, owing US$3 billion.

The loans which these companies had were mainly from Korean banks. Sammi had debts of 430 billion to Korea First Bank, 339 billion to Korea Development Bank, 253 billion to Commercial Bank of Korea, and so on. In turn these banks had borrowed from overseas banks.

Korea First Bank declared losses of 350 billion won in the first six months of 1997. Together, the eight main banks had bad credits of 26 trillion won and were losing annual interest income of 4 trillion. At the beginning of September the government tried to rescue the banks, with special loans from the central bank, the Bank of Korea, to banks and non-bank institutions. Its primary concern was to uphold the reputation of Korean borrowers overseas by protecting depositors.

The banking crisis was caused by these short-term debts, rather than the long-term debt/equity ratios of the major companies, which while high by world standards, had been relatively stable (see Table 1.3).

The Hanbo case was investigated by a parliamentary hearing at which it was alleged that bribes were given by Hanbo to secure loans from the banks. At the subsequent trials of ten people involved in the Hanbo case the president's son Kim Hyun Chul was accused of receiving bribes from Hanbo and other businesses. The managing director of Korea First Bank was found dead, apparently a suicide, during the parliamentary hearings.

analyst was quoted in the London *Times*:[31] 'What you have to realize is that Indonesia is a kleptocracy—Zaire with a bit more civilization. It is run entirely in the interest of the ruling family, who see their large domestic assets threatened with bankruptcy.'

And yet the World Bank President James D. Wolfensohn admitted that the bank had either not realized this or thought that it was not a problem. Speaking in February 1998, he said: 'We miscalculated like the others. When I was here a year ago, I was trapped in Indonesia's enthusiasm. I was not alone in thinking that Indonesia was on the right track.' Peregrine, the Hong Kong-based investment firm, shared the enthusiasm and went bankrupt after lending $260 million to a Jakarta taxi company.

About a fifth of the economy was owned by President Suharto's family, especially his six children who had businesses in almost every sector, including banking, hotels, chemicals, wood, cement, sugar, paper, and toll roads. Foreign investors had to include the family and their connections in their plans before being granted licences to do business. An example of the relationships is provided by the project to build an Indonesian national car. Suharto's son, Hutomo Mandala Putra (also known as 'Tommy'), set up a company to make cars, PT Timor Putra Nasional. The company was given exemption from tariffs and taxes and promptly started importing cars from Korea, rather than building them. $690 million from state-owned banks financed the venture.

Jamsostek (state workers' insurance funds) were used for purposes other than normal investments. In May 1997, the World Bank estimated that 40 per cent of the assets were not accounted for, return on assets was 'virtually nil', and warned of misallocation of funds. A reforestation fund financed by levies from the timber industry, was used to build an aircraft plant for a prominent minister. Iman Tufik, a businessman, said: 'This can't keep going on. How can you have a reforestation fund to pay for a plane. It's crazy.'[32]

One of the conditions of the IMF bail-out was the closure of sixteen banks, three of which were owned by the Suharto family. His middle son, Bambang Trihatmodjo, controlled Bank Andromeda, his middle daughter, Titik Prabowo, controlled Bank Industri, and his half-brother owned Bank Jakarta. His son reopened a branch of his closed banks by buying a licence from another bank.

The World Bank was the biggest single creditor to the Indonesian government. It lent $24.7 billion in the thirty years from 1967. Jeffrey Winters estimated that about $8 billion of this had disappeared, mainly through invoice

Box 3.3 Yamaichi Collapses

On 24 November 1997 Yamaichi Securities, one of Japan's big four stock-brokers went out of business. The Friday before, the day on which the board was meeting to decide how to wind up the company, Moody's Investors Service had downgraded Yamaichi's credit rating to 'speculative'—not a moment too soon.

One reason for its collapse was that it had accumulated hidden losses of Y260 billion, against shareholders' equity of Y100 billion by mid-November. These losses were the result of offering major clients compensation for trading losses. The losses were hidden by transferring loss-making portfolios from client to client so that they did not show up in the relevant accounting period, while guaranteeing paper losses (a practice known as *tobashi*).[1] The company had consistently denied newspaper reports about *tobashi*, as close to the collapse as June 1997, and in 1993 the Securities and Exchange Surveillance Commission had supported such denials. On 24 November Yamaichi President Shohei Nozawa told a news conference that Y158.3 billion of losses were attributable to *tobashi* deals which had begun in 1991.

Another reason for the collapse was the lack of competitiveness of the business. Complacency had led it to miss new business opportunities, such as the new market for dual-currency bonds.

In the run-up to the collapse, Yamaichi ran out of friends. Its main bank, Fuji, refused to make any further loans to bail them out. A year before, Fuji had asked to see Yamaichi's books before making a loan and was refused. By the end the company depended on rolling over Y167 billion in short-term loans and Y160 billion in commercial paper to stay in business.

Yamaichi also ran out of government support. While in the early 1990s the Ministry of Finance did all it could to prevent the collapse of financial institutions, by 1997 that attitude had changed. Sei Nakai, from the Ministry of Finance said in November 1997: 'previous directors-general of the banking bureau thought that their most important task was to prevent bank failures. We made our public believe in the safety of their deposits. But at some time we should have changed that perception gradually. We should have allowed failures and shown how risk operates. This shows we are not so smart.'[2]

Jesper Koll of JP Morgan Securities Asia told *The Age* (Melbourne) 'This is the end of the convoy system. It is an historic turning point; it is the emergence of capitalism in Japan' (27.11.97).

In the months prior to the collapse, Yamaichi did many things to keep up appearances: it spent Y150 billion bailing out its non-bank finance company affiliate; it hired 490 new graduate trainees; in 1996 it moved to a new headquarters building.

1. Such practices were not exclusive to Yamaichi.
2. Quoted in Peter Hartcher, in *The Australian*.

inflation for capital items. Another study, by Professor Sumitro Djojohadi-kusumo, a former finance minister, estimated that about the same propor-tion—30 per cent—of the federal budget disappears each year.

THE END OF RULE BY CONNECTIONS?

We have seen that there are different degrees of integration or separation between the state and business in different countries in the region. Not sur-prisingly, perhaps, party-state–business connections in the PRC make the dis-tinction between the state, the party, and business hardest to define.[33] But, as we saw above, until late 1996, many people, including the *Washington Post*, were not sure whether it mattered. If the purpose is to make money and through that, economic growth, why does it matter that people do business with each other through networks of family and friends rather than through more anonymous and impartial channels? And who cares if you cannot draw a boundary between the state and business? If the police and the army are avail-able to break up a strike or a demonstration, say, is this not good for business? After all, such things have long traditions in Europe and the USA. Such lack of concern was not restricted to US investment in the People's Republic of China. While good returns were to be had, there was no strong objection from 'Western' countries including Australia to the Suharto regime in Indonesia and its connections between the government, the Suharto family, and busi-nesses, nor to logging concessions handed out by Malaysian State rulers to their families. It was not moral objections to the use of family connections and the blurring of boundaries that led outsiders to object to network arrange-ments within a country.

One reason for the objections is that the existence of the sort of trust that develops among families (however defined) excludes outsiders. If loans or investments or supplier deals are made on the basis of connections and are profitable, those without connections are excluded. This was certainly one of the IMF's concerns about Korea's post-crash position. Part of the rescue pack-age was a demand for more openness to foreign ownership, especially in the banking sector. This is especially important for multinational corporations (MNCs) who want to be able to operate anywhere without restriction. One of the first results of the IMF deal in Thailand was the acquisition of Thai banks by US bankers. The abstract idea of free and open markets has underneath the desire of individuals and companies to make money wherever they want to.

A second objection is that even if outsiders are allowed to participate in deals, if the outsider is involved as an underwriter, or a lender to a bank which has control of the final loan conditions, the outsiders will not know what crite-ria are being used in making the loan. If the central bank and government were backing the loan (as they were until very late) in Korea and Japan, then nobody cared—the loan would be repaid. But once lenders had to start making their own risk assessments and decisions, they wanted to know what the criteria for loan-making were. Family connections and a concern for harmony produce different results as decision criteria from risk assessment and cover. Lenders without connections have to rely on the dispassionate assessments that the market provides. A main reason for the insistence by the IMF on improved disclosure (which the IMF calls 'transparency') is the need for such assessments once government underwriting can no longer be relied on. Again, the objection to insider dealing is not a moral one, rather a matter of self-interest in changed circumstances.

More simply, there might be more profit to be made from money lent on economic criteria than on connections. One way of formulating this proposition is this: if the transaction costs of lending and borrowing among strangers are very high, then the trust which comes from network membership might increase profits. At a time of fast economic growth when there are more profitable projects than funds available to invest in them, in a sense, every gamble produces a win.

If the economic criterion is not short-term but long-term profit and growth in market share, then in a sense the 'economic' criteria are less easy to measure. If the intended pay-back period is a generation, or the intended economic outcome is the development of an industrialized nation, the government-backed loans for projects organized among family firms may look perfectly rational and economic. This is another reason for outsiders to object to family-based transactions and may be seen as a clash of cultures. If one partner in a transaction has a very long time-horizon while the other has a very short horizon, they are unlikely to agree on actions.

There are also reasons why people inside the country might object to business being transacted by exclusive networks of families, friends, and classmates. As with foreigners, nationals might also object to being excluded from a network. The case of Taiwan shows how an élite can expand its network to include others without losing control. The KMT managed to incorporate local developing business interests through clientilism, patronage, and politics without losing control of the networks. Had they not done so, it is possible that alternative networks would have developed to challenge those of the KMT.

In the case of Korea, it seems that the excluded finally fought back against the tight family control which had been exercised through the government-bank-*chaebol* network for thirty years. In alliance with the foreigners, the local outsiders managed to benefit from the crisis by having markets and opportunities opened up. The election of Kim Dae Jung was part of the process of expanding access to business beyond the old exclusive élite.

The relationship between democratic politics and patronage may also play a part in the support or otherwise of precapitalist forms of economic transaction. For example, it makes no economic sense for Japan to continue to subsidize rice farmers when consumers benefit from cheaper imported rice. Nor does it make sense for both Japan and Korea to penalize consumers with non-tariff barriers to imports. But it makes good political sense to support local rice-growers and consumer-goods manufacturers.[34]

Obviously anyone who benefits from being a member of an exclusive network which is maintained by connections rather than (especially short-term) profit will have no objections to such 'irrational' transactions. The process of setting up a joint venture is in part one of establishing connections and joining existing networks. Once such membership has been obtained, it then makes sense for the new insiders to object to more outsiders getting connected. The only problem arises when those who are excluded, whether local or foreigners, think that they could benefit from the network being broken into or expanded.

MNCs may or may nor be part of a network. The overseas Chinese network seems to be able to operate across national boundaries, to incorporate relevant parts of national governments, and still operate according to long-term profitability criteria.

There are three, connected reasons for governments or national élites to try to switch their economies from being based mainly on connections to being based mainly on economic rationality. The first is that they are forced to by someone else, whether supranational organizations or foreign investors or lenders. While compliance with outsiders' preferences may be difficult to measure, there are certain aspects of a market economy, such as published accounts and public prices that can be easily demonstrated.

A second reason is that the scale of development requires access to capital from outside the network. While the Chinese diaspora may be able to provide enough capital for rapid growth of Guandong and Fujian provinces in China, other provinces and cities may need access to investors other than their Chinese connections. The unconnected may want to play the game by market rules. Indeed there is evidence that the cost of making connections, including bribery, is a deterrent to some overseas investors.

A third reason may be that a switch from import-substitution to export-led growth leads to the need for more transactions with strangers in importer countries. As in the case of exposure to foreign investment, the opening of trade exposes relationships to influences outside the network rules.

This chapter has shown that there are different sorts of expressive connections in the different countries of the region and a different balance between rule by market and rule by connections. On the surface it looks as if there is a general tendency for the state to withdraw from the economy as state-owned enterprises are privatized and as governments respond to international pressure to introduce more liberal market ways of operating. Government and business, and party-state and business, are still closely connected even in Taiwan, which is now being used by some politicians as the paradigm market economy. In Japan and Korea, the original 'developmental states', there is now a tendency to break up the relationships that sustained the close government–industry links. The main reason for this in Japan is that the connections are no longer good for business and have probably contributed to Japan's long period of slow growth. In Korea the new government, whose members have their own networks, is attacking the old alliances between the government and the *chaebol*. In PRC there is a big switch in economic activity from SOEs to other forms of ownership, some of which are simply alternative forms of collective ownership at local level. In Indonesia and the Philippines there is a tendency to privatize and liberalize state enterprises. While it is clear that there is a tendency towards rule by market so far most of the economies are far from liberal market economies. In the next chapter we ask why there is a tendency towards rule by market and what is the relative importance of globalized trade and investment, the supranational organizations, and domestic politics. The claim by some commentators that the national state is coming to an end of its life is also examined.

NOTES

1. See Chalmers Johnson, *Japan: Who Governs? The Rise of the Developmental State* (New York: Norton, 1995).
2. Ibid. 141.
3. A. Macintyre 'Business, Government and Development: Northeast and Southeast Asian Comparisons', in A. Macintyre (ed.), *Business and Government in Industrialising Asia* (St Leonards, NSW: Allen & Unwin, 1994): 13.
4. Root, *Small Countries, Big Lessons*.
5. Ibid. 17. The statement is more normative than positive: otherwise it would need to explain PRC's inward investment by 'good governance'.
6. Kuo, Cheng-tian, *Global Competitiveness and Industrial Growth in Taiwan and the Philippines* (Pittsburg: University of Pittsburg Press, 1995): 207–8.
7. R. Wade, *Governing the Market: Economic Theory and the Role of Government in East Asian Industrialization* (Princeton: Princeton University Press, 1990).
8. R. Wade, 'Japan, the World Bank, and the Art of Paradigm Maintenance: The East Asian Miracle in Political Perspective', *New Left Review*, 217 (1996).
9. World Bank, *World Development Report* (New York: Oxford University Press, 1997): 1.
10. Ibid. 25–8.
11. Ibid. 25.
12. R. Murphy, *A Dependent Private Sector: No Prospects for Civil Society in China* (Working Paper No. 62, Asia Research Centre, Murdoch University, 1996): 9.
13. Ibid. 25.
14. 1997.
15. A *zaibatsu* is a group of companies in the same ownership that are involved in a number of industries.
16. See W. F. Bello and S. Rosenfeld, *Dragons in Distress: Asia's Miracle Economies in Crisis* (San Francisco: Institute For Food and Development Policy, 1990): 232 and Chang, Ching-hsiu, *Disintegrating KMT Capitalism: A Closer Look at Privatizing Taiwan's State and Party-owned Enterprises* (Taipei: Taipei Society): 1991.
17. Not all of the companies file accounts. The estimate comes from *Asia Week*, 30 June 1997 and *Southeast Asia Business Times*, 6 Feb. 1997.

18. 'The Law on the Organization of Civic Groups'.
19. Quoted in *Topics*, American Chamber of Commerce in Taipei, 1 May 1997.
20. Kuo, *Global Competitiveness*.
21. *Economist*, 14 Oct. 1995: 38.
22. See B. Naughton, 'Chinese Institutional Reform and Privatization From Below', *American Economic Review*, 88/2 (1994).
23. See e.g. Pei X., 'Township-village enterprises, local governments and rural communities: the Chinese village as a firm during economic transition', *Economics of Transition*, 4/1 (1996): 43–66.
24. *Business Week*, 5 Aug. 1997.
25. Figures are hard to come by, especially as the problem is not officially acknowledged. One estimate is that 20% of SOE employees were redundant and being paid in 1997 (*Quest*, 1 May 1997: 30). Many others are not being paid. There are daily reports of demonstrations by unemployed urban workers in north-eastern provinces.
26. Government Information Service (Hong Kong), *Hong Kong's Investment in China* (Hong Kong, 1996).
27. See H. Crouch, *Government and Society in Malaysia* (Ithaca: Cornell University Press, 1996).
28. There is also concern about the consequences of immigration: 'The country should not continue to be over-dependent on foreign workers because of the negative effects it will have in the long-run and the social problems that may arise' (1997 budget speech).
29. 6 Oct. 1996.
30. Korea Development Bank is 100% state-owned, Korea Electric Power Corporation 75%, Korea Telecom 80%, Pohang Iron and Steel 33% and state-managed, for example.
31. 20 Feb. 1998.
32. *Financial Times*, London, 29 Nov. 1997.
33. In 1996 I interviewed a US citizen who had owned a leather garment factory in Shenzhen Special Economic Zone in Guandong, south-east China, for many years. He was planning to move further west to avoid some of the increasing bribes he had to pay in Shenzhen to state officials. He did not understand my questions about state–business relations; 'Doing business in China is doing business with the government.'
34. The same arguments apply to European farm subsidies and US clothing import quotas.

4

The Final Victory of Globalization?

HOMOGENIZATION

When Korea, Indonesia, and Thailand got help from the IMF they had to agree to a list of actions on economic policy, governance issues, and public spending to fit in with the IMF's ideas about how countries should be run. Other countries also came under pressure from lenders and investors to change accounting and disclosure procedures and to make entry and exit to markets easier for foreigners.

Already the free flow of funds and goods around the world had placed countries under universal pressures. The most obvious is on pay levels. Unrestricted trade means that everyone can buy from the cheapest source and high-cost producers have no customers. High-wage economies without tariff and other barriers lose to low-cost competitors. The second influence is on tax rates as companies move their operations to low-tax countries. The consequence of that is that governments try to maintain their tax levels in line with those of their competitors.

Apart from these economic effects of global competition for markets and investment, there are pressures to conform to international accounting standards, open methods of company governance, and 'clean' relationships between business and government. The globalization of markets produces a tendency towards homogenization of market behaviours. At the extreme, these same pressures might homogenize other parts of life, including politics, ideology, and culture. One scenario is that the world adopts the same market economies and liberal politics that currently are said to operate in the USA. The differences in the way governments interact with their economies that we saw in Chapter 3 would eventually disappear. In any case, national governments would do progressively less in the economies. Their policies on other domestic matters such as level of taxation and welfare regimes would also have less scope for difference as the international market determines what is acceptable. Unacceptable behaviour would result in capital flight.

This chapter looks first at the argument that globalization will bring about the end of the nation state. It then looks at the international institutions and asks whether they have the cohesion and power to coerce national governments to conform. Then it asks whether the economic forces of world markets are strong enough to ensure homogeneity of government policies. Finally, it assesses whether there is a future for national politics and national political and economic variety in the global market.

Kenichi Ohmae's book *The End of the Nation State* sets out the argument: capital can establish plants wherever they want to, either for cost or market reasons; government actions, either in tax or regulation, are constrained by the desire not to 'scare away the global economy'.[1] He even argues that China's civil rights policies are constrained by the threat of withdrawal of multinational capital. Ohmae does not claim that these constraints have been accepted by all governments: 'The test for governments of nation states is not whether such pressures arise, but whether they have the will—and the ability—to resist them and to embrace . . . the global economy. . . . the verdict so far is, in most cases, probably not.' But the pressures are irresistible in the long term.

Similarly, Horsman and Marshall argue for the end of the nation state, but not yet: '[the state] has become marginalized by the autonomy of companies operating in the transnational economy'. But the 'global economy' is still in the process of emerging, and has in any event retained links to the system under which it first developed, the world community of nation-states.[2]

The OECD PUMA group[3] adopt a strong version of the effect of globalization: 'There remain few purely "domestic" issues. Competition for international investment—encouraged by the activities and mobility of multinational enterprises—means that most traditionally domestic policies such as education and training, taxation, social protection, economic regulation, or labour legislation, have become international . . . and there are some areas which governments simply cannot control.'[4]

THE SUPRANATIONAL INSTITUTIONS

The International Monetary Fund

The IMF was founded in 1947. Part of its job was to promote 'liberal internationalist' economic policies. These have been described as 'a set of normative preferences for market solutions to economic problems, national economic openness, non-discrimination between nationals and foreigners, and multilateral approaches to common economic challenges'.[5] It is technically an intergovernmental rather than a supragovernmental organization but in practice it can impose its economic policies only on governments weak through borrowing as opposed to those who manage to stay strong despite continuing deficits. Its power is wielded mainly at times when it steps in as lender of last resort, as it did for the three most ailing economies in Asia in 1997. The IMF has 182 member countries.

The IMF claims to have widened its brief from a narrow liberalization agenda when it was founded. At the 1998 annual meeting of the Bretton Woods Committee,[6] Michel Camdessus, managing director of the IMF set out his version of the IMF's policy agenda:

the deregulation of domestic economies and the establishment of a more level playing field for private sector activity, stronger financial systems, and the development of effective regulation and supervision reductions in unproductive government spending, such as costly military build-ups, increased spending on basic human needs, such as primary health and education, on adequate social protection for the poor, the unemployed, and other vulnerable groups, and on key environmental problems, greater transparency and accountability in government and corporate affairs, a more effective dialogue on economic policy with labour and the rest of civil society.

The Association of South-East Asian Nations

ASEAN[7] was founded in 1967 and is more of a club than IMF. Its five founding members declared its objective: 'to create a firm foundation for common action to promote regional cooperation in Southeast Asia in the spirit of equality and partnership and thereby contribute toward peace, progress and prosperity'. In practice it was a genuinely intergovernmental organization and no government has ever sacrificed its country's interests in deference to the good of the region as a whole. Its members agreed that they would not interfere in each other's domestic affairs, although the embarrassment over the internal politics in Myanmar after its admission to the club has generated some diplomatic activity there. ASEAN did little to help in the financial crisis.

Asia Pacific Economic Cooperation (Forum)

APEC has a bigger membership than ASEAN and spans the Pacific. Originally formed in 1989[8] its agenda is similar to that of the IMF—the promotion of liberal policies—rather than forming an exclusive trading block.

World Trade Organization

The WTO was set up in 1994 by most of the members of the General Agreement on Tariffs and Trade. Its member states are party to agreements which are concerned with liberalizing trade. The WTO also intervenes and mediates in trade disputes between nations. Membership requires a commitment to free trade. Whereas GATT was concerned only with trade in goods, the WTO agreements also cover services, such as telecoms and insurance and intellectual property. In 1997 it had 131 members and is an intergovernmental organization.

During 1997 both the PRC and Taiwan started negotiations to join the WTO. The main impact on policy in these places is on their ability to restrict imports either by quotas or tariffs. In Taiwan the industries most likely to be affected are steel and farming, especially meat production. Taiwan's Council of Agriculture estimated that 100,000 jobs in agriculture would be lost as a result of WTO membership.[9]

The governments clearly believe that the benefits of WTO membership exceed the costs. Membership does imply a reversal of the protectionist policies which have helped some industries to develop and survive.

Asian Development Bank

Founded in 1966, the ADB has forty members in the region and sixteen in Europe and North America. It lends money for development, mainly to banks but also for infrastructure, agricultural, and other projects. In 1997 it lent US$9.4 billion. While it has policy stances on matters such as governance, its lending is spread so thinly that it does not wield much power over any individual governments.

As well as these official organizations there are firms of accountants and management consultants as well as banks and other financial institutions that operate around the world. The power of the individual institutions varies and sometimes the volume of funds they control seems to overwhelm national governments.[10] As important is the control they have over the policy options. They are uniformly against public ownership, economic planning, demand management, and rule by connections. They are in favour of privatization, low taxes, and conservative monetary policy.

THE GLOBAL MARKET

Globalized investment?

The Japanese Ministry of International Trade and Industry announced its plan for economic structural reform in May 1997. One of the reasons for reform, said MITI, was that competition was getting harsher:

[A]n era of mega-competition has arrived when economic activity is increasingly globalized and businesses choose countries for better profit and returns on investment as a result of economic development in Asian countries . . . businesses are seeking to operate abroad in a quest for lower costs and optimum production footholds. Manufacturing operations in Japan, as in North American and European countries, are forecasted to be increasingly transplanted abroad in the future.

Such a view is not wholly supported by recent experience. Japan's overseas investment has been made predominantly in Europe and North America. Figure 4.1 shows that over twice as much investment went there as to Asia, most of which was to the PRC. Clearly labour costs and social costs were not the main consideration in locating investment in Europe and North America, rather tariffs and the need for a base in the major markets.

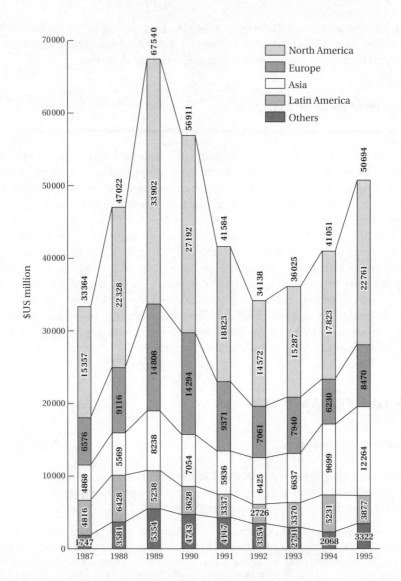

Fig. 4.1 Trends of Japanese direct investment by region

Source: Ministry of Finance, Japan

If we look at the 'stock' of Foreign Direct Investment (FDI) worldwide, we see that most of it is in Europe and North America. Table 4.1 shows that (in 1993) 70 per cent of the stock of FDI was in these two regions but with the rate of flow to China and the rest of Asia accelerating. Mochizuki[11] has shown how Japanese companies intensified their manufacturing investments in East Asia compared with those in the USA after 1989 and that those investments had faster pay-back performance than the US investments. Within Asia, however, such marginal calculations will be relevant. For activities with a relatively high labour content (footwear, garments, some assembly work) 'countries' are in competition with each other for footloose investment and their governments may offer concessions to the investor.

Table 4.1 Stocks and flows of inward and outward FDI by region, 1985 and 1993 ($bn. except where noted)

	Outward stock		Rate of growth (%)	Inward stock		Rate of growth (%)
	1985	1993		1985	1993	
North America	292.5	647.0	9.9	264.1	593.1	10.1
United States	251.0	559.7	10.0	184.6	445.3	11.0
Canada	40.9	86.3	9.3	64.7	106.0	6.2
Mexico	0.5	1.0	8.7	14.8	41.9	13.0
Western Europe	312.3	1,063.9	15.3	242.2	883.5	16.2
EU	286.3	962.0	15.1	223.8	832.1	16.4
Other	23.4	101.8	18.3	18.3	51.4	12.9
South and East Asia						
Japan	44.0	259.8	22.2	4.7	16.9	16.0
Singapore	1.3	6.3	19.7	13.0	50.8	17.0
China	0.1	11.8	56.3	3.4	57.2	35.3
Other	4.2	71.7	35.4	47.9	138.0	13.2
Rest of world	25.0	80.1	14.5	152.6	340.0	10.0
World total	679.4	2,134.6	14.3	727.9	2,079.5	13.1

Source: E. M. Graham, *Global Corporations and National Governments* (Washington: Institute for International Economics, 1996)

If capital is really free to operate where it wants to, why does it continue to employ labour in high-wage economies? While Japanese and Korean manufacturers opened plants in lower-wage economies during the 1980s and early 1990s and opened plants in the USA and Europe to avoid tariff and other barriers to trade, they did not entirely abandon their home manufacturing operations. Similarly, manufacturing continues to operate in high-wage areas such as Australia and Western Europe despite obvious and large cost advantages in the low-wage economies of Asia, especially China, Thailand, and the Philippines. Why, if the world is so globalized and capital so footloose? One answer is that for a plant doing assembly work or any small part of the value chain, wage costs are a small part of total cost. There are additional reasons for organizing production near to markets, including transport costs of the final product, remaining tariffs on imports and non-tariff barriers to imports. Without these factors, all the factories in the world would be in the same place. While this is almost true of very fast-cycle products such as microchips (an industry in which there is room for very few new factories at any one time) it is not true for all.

If the world were really globalized and capital could move where it wanted, then in the long run returns to factors of production would get the same returns wherever they were. This is clearly not the case yet. Market rigidities mean that not only do wage levels vary but returns on investment do too. It is very hard to believe, for example, that wage differences between China and the USA are explained by the differences in labour productivity between those two countries. First, plants built in China are not technically a long way behind those making similar products in the USA. Secondly, if labour productivity in Chinese plants were a small fraction of that in the USA, why build the plants in China in the first place? The reason for the differences lies in the different overall levels of prosperity in the two economies. The minimum level of wages for which it is worth turning up to work is set by local alternative opportunities, not by a global labour market. For wage levels to be equalized there would have to be a very much higher level of labour mobility through migration.

Does this show that keeping labour and social costs low is neither necessary nor sufficient to attract FDI? The answer depends on the reasons for companies making investments in countries other than their home base. If they are looking for a local base near the market, as must be the case for Japanese investment in North America and Europe, then the relevant comparators are Canada and the USA and within-Europe. There is no need for governments in these regions to compete with Thailand or Indonesia in wage or social costs. If investors are looking for low labour-cost locations, then they will obviously avoid North America and Europe in favour of very low-cost locations. Adjusting labour protection or social wage contributions at the margin will not materially alter the costs.

Gerald Epstein[12] has argued that domestic investment depends very much on the level of domestic savings although capital flight can be caused by loss of international confidence in a national economy. The 1997/8 crisis rather emphasized the latter point as portfolio investment was withdrawn rapidly from a range of national stock markets. There is a difference between the mobility of portfolio investment and that of direct investment, especially in the short term. It is easier to realize the value of a paper asset than that of a factory. As investment cycles get shorter and investments have a shorter life, this is less true. Companies can build factories with tax concessions, favourable loans, and subsidized land and leave them relatively quickly.

The local economy

All countries have a non-traded sector which, in principle, is protected from global competition. Table 4.2 shows the relative sizes of the agricultural, manufacturing, and service sectors. Not all services are free from overseas competition but there is a core which must be carried out locally such as healthcare, education, retail banking, and entertainment. As economies grow an increasing proportion of consumption and production occurs in the service sector. Table 4.2 shows that the world service industries account for 63 per cent of world GDP.

Table 4.2 Share of value added in GDP of agriculture, industry, and services

	Agriculture	Industry	Services
China	21	48	31
Indonesia	17	42	41
Philippines	22	32	46
Thailand	11	40	49
Malaysia	13	43	44
Korea	7	43	50
Hong Kong	0	17	83
Singapore	0	36	64
Japan	2	38	60
World	5	33	63

Source: World Development Report 1997: 236–7

Globalized trade?

When we look at the pattern of trade in the region, we see that rather than an even flow of goods between the countries there are some strong ties between nations and others which are very weak. Figure 4.2 shows exports from the countries in the region in 1995. Trade between Hong Kong and the rest of China amounted to the biggest flows, $57 billion from the PRC to HK and $36 billion from HK.[13] The Japan–China trade is the next largest, with $25 billion and $29 billion of exports, followed by Japan's exports to Indonesia and Korea's to Japan. What is striking is how small the other trade flows are in comparison. Apart from Indonesia's exports (mainly of primary products) to Japan, the trade flows from Thailand, Malaysia, and the Philippines are small. However, as a proportion of GDP, exports from these countries is higher than European or North American levels.

Table 1.2 showed imports and exports for a selection of countries in the region as a percentage of GDP. If openness, in the sense of dependency on overseas markets, creates pressures for convergence, then clearly there are great pressures in this region, except in the case of Japan which has a relatively

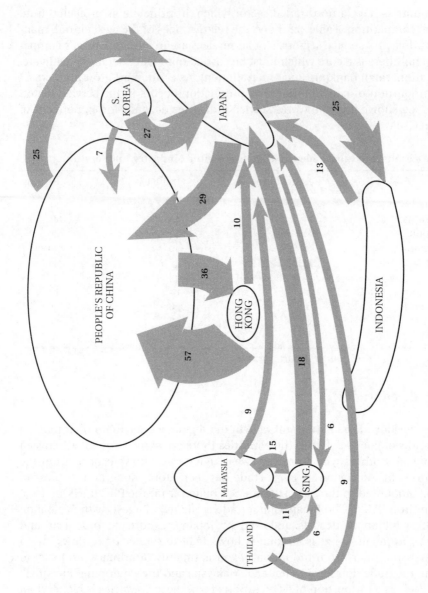

Fɪɢ. 4.2 **Exports within the region, 1995**
Source: Table 4.3

closed economy, exports and imports together accounting for 18 per cent of GDP. When we look at the destination of exports in Table 4.3, we see that these relatively open economies are mainly exporting to USA, Japan, Singapore, and Hong Kong. Over half of Malaysia's exports go to these four places, 62 per cent of the PRC's, 50 per cent of Indonesia's, and 53 per cent of Thailand's. They are competing with each other in these markets, as low-cost production locations.

The impact of trade and investment on the relative autonomy of national governments depends on the governments' relative strength. First, how powerful is local business compared with foreign businesses? If local business relies on world markets for equity investments or loans, national governments have less scope for autonomy. Second, has the government sufficient domestic support for 'national' policies? If local capital benefits from globalization, for example in keeping workers' wage demands down, governments will be in a poor position to step out of line with global trends. This is linked to the third question of power balance: how strong is local labour organization in response to demands for equalized wages and working conditions? Fourth, how dependent is the domestic government on loans from international institutions able to impose loan conditions?

GLOBALIZATION AS POWER STRUGGLE

Globalization is an idea promoted by forces that stand to gain from the freer flow of capital and international competition among workers. There are some powerful countervailing forces. First there are national owners of businesses who stand to lose from global capital flows, including having their assets bought in hostile takeovers. Unless governments abandon sovereignty of their territories the collection of companies in a country can be represented by the state. 'Malaysia Inc.' or 'Japan Inc.' are more than slogans: they represent a national interest which is seen as the sum of the interest of national companies, possibly including their workers. These interests have been protected from competition by tariffs and subsidies and other barriers to trade, all of which are threatened by liberalization. They may also be protected in domestic markets by measures to discourage foreign investment. The main reason for restrictions on the businesses which foreigners could enter in Indonesia was to protect local interests. Taiwan had limits of foreign share ownership. China has a controlled system of foreign investment and joint ventures.

Governments also have reasons to maintain sovereignty apart from protecting the interests of local businesses. Governments or parties derive their legitimacy mostly from their ability to define and represent a 'national' interest. In Japan the LDP and civil service gained most of their legitimacy from their identification with the national interest of economic growth for thirty years. UMNO in Malaysia created a nation and tried to emulate Japan's success by copying state–business relationships. The KMT had to create a state in

Table 4.3 Trade patterns, 1995 (US$m.)

	PRC	Malaysia	Philippines	Indonesia	Singapore	Korea	Hong Kong	Thailand
Exports, 1995								
USA	24,744	15,216	6,216	7,223	17,537	24,343	37,851	10,227
Japan	28,466	9,334	2,760	12,908	6,224	17,014	10,596	9,303
Singapore	3,500	14,890	993			6,580	4,922	7,750
United Kingdom	2,791	2,937	910	1,292	3,056	2,930	5,584	1,594
Hong Kong	36,003	3,798	825	1,485	9,172	10,387		2,779
Netherlands	3,233	1,724	785	922	1,582		2,825	1,628
Thailand		2,785	736		5,808			
Germany	5,672	2,363	700	1,760	3,165	2,965	7,491	1,723
S. Korea	6,688	2,073	426	3,021	2,081		2,804	1,033
France			206				2,666	
Australia				996				
Malaysia				1,092	11,066	2,967		2,267
Russia	1,674							
Italy	2,068							
PRC		1,997		1,866	3,089	9,517	57,861	
Indonesia						2,969		
Panama						2,626		
Canada							2,633	
Belg.-Lux.								738
Saudi Arabia								
New Zealand								
Iran								
TOTAL	148,755	73,641	17,318	43,007	88,497	126,494	173,546	56,920

Imports, 1995

USA	16,123	12,448	5,130	3,730	16,761	30,271	14,882	7,620
Japan	29,007	20,866	6,367	10,966	25,306	32,845	28,602	21,761
Singapore	3,398	9,664	1,290	884	3,542		10,089	4,165
United Kingdom		2,188	566				3,936	1,446
Hong Kong	8,599		1,452	1,168	5,438			
Netherlands								
Thailand		2,005			7,942		2,728	
Germany	8,035	3,482	990	2,946	4,015	6,680	4,142	3,734
S. Korea	10,288	3,184	1,400	3,267	7,162		9,472	2,604
France	2,649	2,236		1,139				1,756
Australia	2,586	2,053	814	1,911		4,919		1,357
Malaysia			604	1,041	17,090	2,475	3,723	3,020
Russia	3,799							
Italy	3,116					2,410	3,573	
PRC		1,747		1,582	3,850	7,751	69,737	2,028
Saudi Arabia			1,697		3,960	5,379		
Indonesia						3,324		
Canada						2,546		
Netherlands								
New Zealand								
Iran								
TOTAL	132,007	76,999	28,284	39,211	121,456	135,925	192,764	69,761

Source: Asian Development Bank, *Key Indicators*, xvii (1996)

Taiwan. Governments and parties whose reason for being is the nation do not willingly surrender national sovereignty to impersonal forces of 'globalization'. Of course there are contradictions in this position: sovereign states wishing to attract foreign investment face competition from other sovereign states.

There are workers who are in a position to resist the wage and benefit cuts implied in the competition for jobs. The 1997/8 resistance by the Australian wharf workers in New South Wales and Victoria is a good example of an organized workforce resisting strong pressure from both employers and federal and state governments to reduce their wages and remove their employment protection in the name of globalization. In the process, by keeping wharf costs high they protected workers in other industries from imports as a substitute for domestically made products, such as steel. Workers in Korea used traditional methods such as strikes and demonstrations to resist reductions in their working conditions to 'world' standards.

Another source of resistance to globalization is the fact that the rest of the world is not a free-trade area but a set of trading blocs with their own protective arrangements. This provides arguments, at least, against abandoning all domestic protection against their trading partners in Europe and North America.

Pressure from supra-national institutions is dependent on the power balance between the victim nation and the other members. Such power shifts with national economic fortunes. Only when countries need to borrow do they have to submit to international policy pressure. If China's banks had been more exposed to foreign depositors and lenders in 1997, the government would have had to make a reform of its banking and bank regulations system similar to that of Thailand and Indonesia.

Despite these reservations about the strength of the impact on national governments of capital's ability to set up its operations anywhere, the argument has been taken up rhetorically by many governments to justify their actions towards public services. The Australian government justified the introduction of more 'flexible' employment terms for the Australian Public Service by reference to 'building a competitive economy'.[14] The former French government made similar claims: 'the opening of the borders exposes all our collective functions to international competition. It is time that the state, in its turn, changes its habits and works with current methods.'[15]

The 'end-of-the-nation-state-because-of-globalization' argument has also been used to justify reductions in welfare spending, for example under the Mitterand government in France, in New Zealand, and Australia. Global competition was used by the Chinese government as a reason for not increasing old-age pensions in Hong Kong, arguing that increasing the pension from US$128 per month would threaten Hong Kong's competitiveness. Employers bargaining with their workers also use 'globalization'. Workers have to accept lower pay unless they want their company to move to a lower-wage area or lose in price competition to companies already operating in low-wage areas.

Mishra says that the globalization argument is an excuse to take many matters out of national politics: 'Globalization . . . appears as an external constraint—not a matter of political choice at all, but rather of economic necessity—so that nation-states can do little besides follow the dictates of footloose capital in a downward spiral of deregulation, lower social spending and lower taxes.'[16]

If all governments were to 'embrace' globalization, they would eventually have similar policies both about the role of the state (and the taxation levels implied by that role) and the way in which the state is financed and managed. There would be a form of negative auction in which governments compete for the favours of transnational investors. One of the mechanisms through which international capital ensures a convergence of policies from national governments is through supranational or transnational organizations. Supranational organizations are those to which nation states have delegated some of the powers they might previously have exercised internally. Free-trade associations such as NAFTA or the EU have bureaucracies which implement policies agreed by their constituent nation states and eventually take on a policy-making life of their own. One interpretation of these developments is that they are the early stages of a confederation—free-trade zones being precursors to more power being devolved 'upwards' from the nation state, in the way that modern Germany developed into a nation state for example.

WHAT IS LEFT FOR THE STATE?

Whether the scenario of homogenization through globalization turns out to be real depends on the dynamic between the international markets and institutions and national politics. National politicians use 'globalization' as a justification for their policies. Opposition to low taxes is countered by reference to the impact on inward investment. Protectionist lobbies are told that tariffs are unacceptable to the World Trade Organization. Trade unions' demands for employment guarantees are rejected on the grounds of the need for flexibility in global markets. How the dynamic is played out depends on the strength and cohesiveness of the supranational institutions and their political backers, the relative impact of markets themselves, for labour, goods and services, and capital, and the extent to which national governments are willing and able to stand up to these pressures. That willingness will depend on whether the national élites' interests are met or not by homogenization and whether other interests, whether workers, farmers, or employers, can maintain some degree of protection.

Linda Weiss[17] has argued that globalization has not led to homogenization of policy and the decline of state power. Her argument is that globalization has been exaggerated and that the impact on the autonomy and power of national governments has been less than that claimed by many commentators. On the effects of world trade, she points out that the proportion of national GDPs which is traded is declining as non-traded services make up a higher proportion of GDP when economies grow. The impact of transnational investment is also exaggerated: much FDI is in non-productive activities such as hotels and golf courses; FDI is normally less than 10 per cent of a nation's total investment. She also argues that the truly transnational corporation is a rarity and its powers are limited. On the state, she argues that governments have adapted to changing patterns of trade and investment and in some cases, such as Japan, Taiwan, and Korea have promoted internationalization. She concludes

[C]onvergence towards a neoliberal model of political economy is highly improbable. This is not simply because economic 'globalization' is rather more limited and subject to counter-tendencies than many accounts would suggest. It is also because nation-states themselves exhibit great adaptability and variety—both in their responses to change and in their capacity to mediate and manage domestic linkages, in particular the government–business relationship.[18]

Susan Strange, in a study of alternatives to state power in the world, is sceptical about the willingness of national governments to give up their autonomy to intergovernmental organizations: 'Realists in and out of government, the universities and the media are confirmed in their scepticism about the readiness of states to concede real authority and independent legitimacy to inter-governmental committees and assemblies.'[19] Even the IMF's powers are limited, she argues, if the countries which fall out of line can manage to raise funds internationally without recourse to the fund. However, she also showed that the power of nation states was being eroded by a variety of other institutions and groupings, including organized crime, accounting firms, and cartels of private businesses.

These arguments agree with Robert Wade[20] that the death of the nation state has been exaggerated. A high proportion of production in most countries is for domestic consumption. Those countries that have very high levels of imports and exports relative to national production have high volumes of trade in goods that are imported and re-exported. Wade also argues that there are few genuinely international corporations, rather there are companies based in one state with production and distribution facilities in other countries. An additional argument is that when governments make policy to attract inward investment they often use special export-processing zones (Indonesia, Philippines, Thailand for example) or special economic zones (PRC) where there are different levels of taxes, regulations, and labour rights. In other words, there may be a negative auction for these zones while a different set of rules applies in the rest of the country. The zones are a relatively small proportion of the whole national economy. The two most footloose industries are assembly of electronic goods and manufacture of clothing and footwear. Governments can choose whether to adjust regulatory welfare and tax policies to attract these industries.

China has had a very large influx of FDI, especially to the coastal areas. It has done this partly by making sure that there is a hard-working and uncomplaining workforce. The Singapore government decided to concentrate on FDI for its economic development and has succeeded in attracting regional corporate headquarters as well as manufacturing plants. It has done it by creating an economy and a society attractive to corporations.

But there is nothing special about foreign investment in wanting and benefiting from a docile workforce and low taxes. Domestic capital also benefits from the competitive advantage so provided. When that capital is closely linked to those in government (or even owned by them), then it is the same individuals who put the policies in place as benefit from them. Both Japan and Korea have loosened their labour protection policies, not to attract inward investment but to give domestic manufacturers more power to lay off workers to cut costs or cut production during the downturn.

Globalization and the attraction of footloose investment may be an excuse, therefore, rather than an overriding reason for the suppression of workers' rights. It may be easier to justify long hours, low pay and poor conditions by reference to an overriding need to attract overseas investors than to boost the competitiveness of domestic producers. The impact on the workers is the same: international competition based on labour costs leads to downward pressure on wages and conditions everywhere, whoever owns the production facilities. In the cases of Japan and Korea, workers are competing against the workers in the countries in which their companies are investing. The workers in Thailand, Vietnam, or Indonesia are competing against their Korean and Japanese counterparts. The intergovernmental organizations are not strongly involved in this aspect of national competitiveness. What they (and especially the IMF) stress is access to markets, both for products and investment. Restrictions on such access are removed whenever they get a chance to intervene.

A major constraint would occur if there were ever a government elected in any of these states that had a radically different policy from the consensual free-market approach. A government that decided to take into state ownership either domestic or foreign-owned firms would be in a very difficult position and would provoke reaction from many sources. So would a newly created protectionist policy for new industries. WTO and individual retaliation would make such policies difficult to implement. The policies of industrial promotion, the creation of industries through state enterprises, and restrictions on imports to protect domestic industries would not be possible in countries subscribing to WTO rules and wanting foreign capital. The strategies that were adopted by Japan and Korea are no longer an option.

In other words, the effects of globalization only look weak because the states involved are currently following similar polices towards liberalization of markets, albeit to different degrees. It is only when some of them step out of the dominant liberal line that we would see a strong reaction. Japan and Indonesia are examples of states which are far from this model. Whenever there is an economic problem, the international community, represented whether by intergovernmental organizations or by individual governments, tries to get them to fall into line. The question is how far will these efforts be successful? How strong are the networks of expressive ties in their resistance to rule by market criteria in these countries? Once the economic crisis has passed and the banks and governments have less need to convince foreigners of their compliance with market rules, will the previous ways of operating return? In the case of the PRC, the market rules are only loosely applied. State planning, party-state controlled banking, land allocation, licensing, and regulation are very different from a liberal economy.

How governments use their remaining discretion and autonomy still depends on local politics. The arguments about labour protection, environmental degradation, and safety standards in factories may take place in international forums such as the International Labour Organization but the day-to-day bargaining takes place within a context of local politics. When Japanese logging companies cut down the rainforests in South-east Asia for building materials in Japan, they were not simply abstract agents of some global market place. They had to negotiate with tribal communities who lived in the forests, with local and province-level politicians, and with national governments in the states in which they operated. There was nothing inevitable about the destruction of the forests, rather that the people who used to live in them were less powerful than those who benefited from their destruction. The

---

Box 4.1 Nike

Nike, the USA-based sports shoe and sportswear company, became the subject of critical attention for the wages and conditions in its Asian factories. The National Labour Committee reported in March 1998 on conditions in twenty-one Chinese factories making products for four major US manufacturers: 'We found forced overtime, 60–96 hour weeks, 10–15 hour shifts six and seven days a week for below-subsistence wages.' Nike denied the charges, saying that at one of the factories, at Yue Yein, average wages were $77.75 per month, well above the minimum of $41.86. In its factory built on the former Long Binh US military base at Tae Kwang, Vietnam, 8,800 workers earn $1.5 per day and make half a million shoes a month.

Nike employs 350 subcontractors in thirty-three countries who in turn employ 450,000 people to make its products. The Asian subcontractors are mainly owned by Koreans and Taiwanese and operate factories in China, Indonesia, and Vietnam. Nike has a turnover of nearly $10 billion. In 1997 the company sold 200,000,000 pairs of shoes. Towards the end of 1997 sales faltered and the company cancelled contracts with contractors, resulting in 50,000 job losses.[1]

1. *The Oregonian*, Portland, 19 Nov. 1997.

same applies to factory conditions, child labour, and minimum pay levels. In principle, there is no reason why a state or local government could not simply say 'no' to Nike. The fact that few do is not evidence that no government is ever able to control local conditions because of the forces of global capitalism, rather that governments generally choose to go with the flow of the market and plead inevitability.

GLOBAL GOVERNANCE FOR A GLOBAL ECONOMY?

It is clear that many aspects of the economy are now beyond the control of national governments. The crisis ended the period of the dollar peg for many of the Asian currencies, as their reserves proved inadequate to combat the reserves controlled by the speculators. The Multinational Agreement on Investment further takes away national conditionality on inward investment. Membership of the WTO restricts the degree to which governments can control trade flows and protect domestic producers. Investment flows can generate a negative auction of labour costs and labour and welfare rights.

This loss of control represents a change in the balance of governance, from rule by law and regulation to rule by the market at the international level. Advocates of the market would applaud this development, on the grounds that it will eventually raise total world production. Detractors would point to the destructive impact of unregulated markets, in the way that Keynes advocated state intervention to reduce the destructive impact of the economic cycle. In recent years the frequent currency crises have also had a destructive impact on real economies and on people's well-being throughout the world.

It is unlikely that any of the existing international institutions would be capable of running global counter-cyclical fiscal and monetary policy even if they thought that trying to moderate the cycle was feasible. The national governments are unlikely to give up their remaining policy instruments, fiscal and monetary policy. But is there any chance of a supranational rule of law in relation to other destructive aspects of the global market? We saw in Chapter 2 that there were two immediate causes of the economic crisis in Asia: the attack on the currencies by speculators and the rapid outflow of portfolio investment funds. Would it be possible to impose some supranational control on these forces?

Before the debate about international controls on speculation began in 1997, I. G. Patel had proposed that the IMF could intervene:

I have often wondered why the combined power of national Central Banks and the IMF cannot be marshaled on occasion to combat speculative pressures. Why should the resources of the IMF not be enlarged and used for countering speculation, as distinguished from meeting a balance-of-payments deficit? The IMF could usefully enter into some profitable business with its richer members by creating a facility which could be quickly drawn upon by a Central bank to supplement its reserves when the Central

Bank and the IMF are agreed that it is desirable to combat speculation against a currency.[21]

Whether this would work would depend on the balance of funds available to the particular central bank and the IMF on the one hand and the combined funds of the speculators on the other. Whether it would be desirable would depend on whether the exchange rates being defended were defensible in the long-term fundamentals of the currencies' economy.

A less global multinational solution would be a regional currency union. When the 1997 crisis broke, one suggestion made by Mahatir Mohammed was that the ASEAN countries try to reduce their dependency on US dollars as a medium of exchange. One way to do that, he suggested, was barter settlement of bills. In the event this proved too difficult since there was little simple balanced trade between two countries which could be financed in this way and in any case the businesses involved in trade needed cash for their products. However, there could be a regional monetary union in which rates are pegged or allowed to vary within defined bands and a currency in which local trade is conducted. It would be harder for speculators to attack a currency representing ASEAN countries or a wider grouping than to attack a single currency. This would require a new institution to manage the combined currency. It is not clear that either ASEAN or APEC in their current form would generate the trust from national governments to hand over a degree of national autonomy. Without such an arrangement, however, they have given up their autonomy to the abstract 'market forces' that produced the crisis. It would go some way towards controlling short-term capital flows: if investors have confidence in the exchange rate, they are less likely to indulge in panic selling. There still might be some merit in making some controls over short-term capital movements which would be easier to implement if there were some international agreement about how the controls should operate. The control would be similar to existing rules in some stock markets that stop trading after a certain percentage change in prices in a trading session.

So far, all supranational or international organizations have pursued polices of liberalization that have been accepted with varying degrees of enthusiasm. The IMF and the World Bank together with the World Trade Organization have dominated official policy debate on how economies should be run and how the world economy should function. Events in Japan and Korea have been used to further promote the liberal position and deny the value of rule by connections. There are three counter-arguments to this position. The economic crisis would have been less severe if there had been some regulation of short-term international capital flows. Adjustments in stock market and foreign exchange levels might have done less damage to unemployment and income levels if they had been less dramatic. The second argument is that national governments were prevented from treating the recession with proper counter-cyclical measures because of the IMF's insistence on raising interest rates and cutting government spending. Governments may not be willing to continue to implement 'one size fits all' economic policies once their populations react to those policies' dire consequences. The third counter-argument is that those countries that did least badly in the crisis were not necessarily those that followed the liberal line. The most obvious case is the PRC, which managed to maintain high growth and is probably the most controlled economy in the region with regard to investment flows and foreign exchange dealings. Taiwan is another example of an economy with considerable government steering despite its growing image as a liberal economy. Even Hong Kong, for long the bastion of the market, saved its markets from worse collapse by government intervention in foreign exchange and stock markets and manipulation of the property market.

NOTES

1. K. Ohmae, *The End of the Nation State: The Rise of Regional Economies* (London: HarperCollins, 1995): 75.
2. M. Horsman and A. Marshall, *After the Nation-State* (London: HarperCollins, 1994): 235.
3. OECD Public Management Service, *Globalisation: What Challenges and Opportunities for Governments?* (Paris: OECD, 1996).
4. Ibid. 2. Hirst and Thompson (1996) argue that both trade and investment have been more global in previous periods: P. Hirst and G. Thompson, *Globalization in Question* (Cambridge: Polity Press, 1996).
5. L. W. Pauly, 'Promoting a Global Economy: The Normative Role of the International Monetary Fund', in R. Stubbs and G. R. D. Underhill (eds.), *Political Economy and the Changing Global Order* (New York: St Martin's Press, 1994): 204.
6. 13 Feb. 1998 in Washington, DC.
7. It has nine members: Thailand, Brunei, Indonesia, Malaysia, Philippines, Singapore, Vietnam, Myanmar (Burma), and Laos. There is a plan to create a free-trade area among the members to eventually reduce tariffs on manufactured goods to 5% maximum.
8. The first ministerial meeting had representatives from Brunei Darussalam, Canada, Indonesia, Japan, S. Korea, Malaysia, New Zealand, Philippines, Singapore, Thailand, and Australia. The PRC, Hong Kong, and Taiwan joined in 1991 and they were joined in 1993 by Mexico and Papua New Guinea and in 1994 by Chile. Peru, Russia, and Vietnam will bring the membership to twenty-one. For a summary of APEC's origins see: W. Bodde, *View from the 19th Floor; Reflections of the First APEC Executive Director* (Singapore: Institute of Southeast Asian Studies, 1994).
9. Central News Agency (Taiwan), 9 Mar. 1998.
10. For a pessimistic view, see Hans-Peter Martin and Harald Schuman, *The Global Trap: Globalization and the Assault on Democracy and Prosperity* (London: Zed Books, 1997).
11. M. M. Mochizuki, Japan as an Asia-Pacific Power', in R. S. Ross (ed.), *East Asia in Transition: Toward a New Regional Order* (Armonk, NY: M. E. Sharpe, 1995).

12. G. Epstein, 'International Capital Mobility and the Scope for National Economic Development', in R. Boyer and D. Drache (eds.), *States Against Markets: The Limits of Globalisation* (London, New York: Routledge, 1996).
13. These figures reflect the fact that a large proportion of China's exports and imports are routed through Hong Kong.
14. P. Reith, 'Towards a Best Practice Australian Public Service', discussion paper (Minister for Industrial Relations, Canberra, 1996): 5.
15. Quoted in N. Flynn and F. Strehl (eds.), *Public Sector Management in Europe* (London: Prentice-Hall Harvester Wheatsheaf, 1996): 123.
16. M. Mishra, 'The Welfare of Nations', in R. Boyer and D. Drache (eds.), *States Against Markets: The Limits of Globalisation* (London, New York: Routledge, 1996): 317.
17. L. Weiss, *The Myth of the Powerless State: Governing the Economy in a Global Era* (Cambridge: Polity, 1998) and L. Weiss, 'Globalization and the Myth of the Powerless State', *New Left Review*, 225 (Sept.–Oct. 1997).
18. Weiss, *The Myth of the Powerless State*: 26.
19. S. Strange, *The Retreat of the State: The Diffusion of Power in the World Economy* (Cambridge: Cambridge University Press, 1996): 184.
20. R. Wade, 'Globalization and its Limits: Reports of the Death of the National Economy are Greatly Exaggerated', in S. Berger and R. Dore (eds.), *National Diversity and Global Capitalism* (Ithaca: Cornell University Press, 1996).
21. I. G. Patel, 'Global Economic Governance: Some Thoughts on Our Current Discontents', in M. Desai and P. Redfern (eds.), *Global Governance: Ethics and Economics of the World Order* (London: Pinter, 1995): 29.

Democracy, the Economy, and the Crisis

Proponents of liberal democracy have seen a relationship between the growth of output and the growth of democracy. There are two arguments. The first is that as economies develop new classes grow, especially of professionals, white-collar workers, and small business owners. The new classes are said to react against authoritarianism and demand a voice in the way in which their societies are run. A typical proponent of the argument is Helliwell[1] in an article which presents correlations between growth rates and indices of democracy. He says in his conclusion: 'It is relatively uncontentious to suggest that increasing levels of education and income are likely to increase citizen demands for many things, including the range of political and civil freedoms that characterize democratic systems.'

Samuel Huntington[2] said that there was a 'third wave' of democratic development between 1974 and 1989, following the first and second waves in the nineteenth century and following the Second World War. Huntington defined countries as either democratic or not and counted the increase in the numbers in the former category.

An extreme version of the argument says that there is no alternative to what happens in 'the West', which is defined as liberal democracy. Fukuyama has argued that the collapse of the communist regimes in Eastern Europe means that the whole world will converge by establishing liberal democratic systems and such political systems are the natural consequence of capitalism. In his book *Trust*,[3] he argues that central planning is inadequate to generate growth and that growth is good for democracy:

The enormous prosperity created by technology-driven capitalism, in turn, serves as an incubator for a liberal regime of universal and equal rights, in which the struggle for recognition of human dignity culminates. . . . the world's advanced economies have no alternative model of political and economic organization other than democratic capitalism.[4]

He later argues that 'social capital' (defined as the capacity for self-organization) leads to the development of markets and 'the market can in fact play a role as a school of sociability that reinforces democratic institutions'.[5]

An opposite argument was applied in Asia. One version is the 'Asian values' explanation. The individualism implied by elections and the confrontation implied by competition between parties contradict the values of collectivism and harmony. A Taiwanese politician put the case, which has been articulated by many others including Lee Kuan Yew of Singapore, Tung Chee Hwa in Hong Kong and to some extent by Mahatir Mohammad[6] in Malaysia:

[B]ecause democracy is a foreign import and it needs to operate under Taiwan's Chinese socio-cultural traditions, there are inevitable contradictions and tensions that would affect its structural underpinnings and effectiveness . . . the notion of a participatory pluralist society where an actively involved citizenry compete for favorable policy outcomes by open, frequently hostile confrontation appears peculiar to most Chinese on Taiwan.[7]

The other counter-argument is based on the observed behaviours of the emerging classes. Increasing income leads to a desire to retain wealth and to a political conservatism. The middle classes have no obvious interest in either liberal politics or a democratic society. While some students and workers' representatives may see democracy as the way to promote their interests, the newly emerging middle classes have different interests. This is especially the case where the rising classes belong to ethnic minorities who are either excluded or exclude themselves from the political process, especially the Chinese business and trading classes in South-east Asia[8].

It is clearly the case that the last twenty-five years have produced many aspects of democratization in the region. China cannot be described as democratic, despite developments of elected bodies in rural areas although politics involves lengthy processes of consultation and consensus-building, nor can Singapore despite the elections to the legislature. Indonesia was governed by the military and the ruling family. Elsewhere, there is a trend away from authoritarianism. Authoritarian regimes were replaced in Korea in 1988 and in the Philippines in 1992. In 1996 Taiwan had its first presidential election at which the incumbent president Lee Teng-hui was reappointed. Hong Kong has an element of democracy in the election of its legislature if not the government. Malaysia's ruling UMNO party does not have a monopoly of power. Thai governments had been elected since 1992. An election has been called in Indonesia after a long period of military and oligarchic rule.

On the face of it, the region is becoming more democratic. Fidel Ramos, the former president of the Philippines, made a speech in December 1998,[9] in which he said that in the political sphere the age of authoritarian rule by force in the region was at an end, citing the elections held in rural areas in China as well as the end of authoritarian rule in Thailand, Indonesia, South Korea, and the Philippines in the past twenty years. Even in the PRC there are well-publicized elections in the rural areas which have led visitors, including President Clinton, to express optimism about the future of democracy there. Is there really a convergence towards a democratic system to eventually make East and South-east Asia indistinguishable from Europe and North America? Or are there special characteristics of these societies that produce fundamentally different political systems?

DEMOCRACY AND THE CRISIS

First we ask what light the economic crisis throws on the state of democracy in the region. When people believed in the 'miracle' thesis, a degree of authoritarianism was said to be an essential or at least useful attribute for economic growth. If the government was to direct economic development, the process would be faster and more efficient if it were not slowed down by democratic accountability and the lobbying and debate that went with it. At a diplomatic level even quite repressive regimes, such as the military dictatorships in Korea and Indonesia, were supported by the USA and other governments as long as they were not communist and produced economic growth.

One of the international responses to the crisis was the call for greater openness and accountability of governments. The argument was that the bad loans and negative results of 'cronyism' could only happen because they were hidden from view. Such arguments, especially by the IMF, separated the issue of accountability from that of democracy. Investors want accountability through disclosure rules and internationally accepted accounting standards. Accountability and openness through democratic institutions are a separate issue and of limited interest to investors and especially foreign investors. In principle these two aspects of openness are different as the government sphere may be separated from business. Elected representatives scrutinizing government spending and actions are different from stockholders' relationships with the companies in which they invest. Here we are concerned with the impact of the political regime on the crisis and of the crisis on the democratic process. Did democracy affect the degree to which countries were affected by the crisis? Did the crisis affect the move towards democracy?

Figure 1.2 showed the degree of collapse of equity prices. The least badly affected by the end of August 1998 were Taiwan and Hong Kong. The most dramatic drops were in Indonesia and Thailand. A middle group consisted of Singapore, the Philippines, Malaysia, and Korea. Whatever else the markets reacted to, it was clearly not the degree of democracy in the countries[10]. Compared with Hong Kong, Taiwan has more of the features of democracy including a popularly elected assembly and president, although it is still ruled by the KMT. At the other end of the scale of collapse, Thailand and Indonesia had different democratic attributes, the military being more firmly in command in Indonesia than Thailand. Both markets fell more than 85 per cent. Of course the reasons for the degree of market collapse were based in the economic fundamentals and the 'sentiment' of investors. The point is that the degree of democracy did not seem to affect the degree of overvaluation or the scale of the 'correction' during 1997/8.

DEMOCRACY AND THE ECONOMY

In the longer run, democracy may be associated with economic growth. If it is the case that networks allocate resources less efficiently than markets, then a society based on expressive network ties will be less rich than one based on dispassionate economic calculation. The question is, therefore, whether the development of democracy has reduced the power of the patronage networks. In other words has the spread of democratic institutions produced a more liberal society in the sense that economic agents are allowed to operate without having to be a part of an expressive network based on personal, family, or geographical connections?

Examples might provide some answers to this question. First we look at Taiwan which should provide a paradigm case of the move from authoritarianism to democracy. Second we turn to Korea, an example of a military regime turned democratic, then Malaysia, which has been called 'semi-authoritarian' or 'authoritarian populist'.[11] The crisis showed Indonesia as the paradigm case of 'crony capitalism' as the Suharto regime's business interests became clear. The Philippines has a history of democratic elections since the end of martial law in 1986.

Taiwan

Taiwan should provide an example of the transition from an authoritarian state with a large state-owned enterprise sector and political patronage to an elected democracy and free market. Taiwan held its first presidential election in March 1996, the first direct election of a provincial president in China's history, in which President Lee Teng-hui was confirmed in office. There is no doubt that having to face elections caused the ruling Kuomintang to respond to demands for more freeedom and democracy. How did Taiwan change from an authoritarian regime, which had been ruled by martial law for the forty years until 1988, to an apparently democratic one?

The Kuomintang moved to Taiwan after its defeat by the Communist Party in 1947 to establish what it called the Republic of China. Because the KMT believed that their government was the legitimate authority in the whole of China, they established a provincial tier of government as if Taiwan were one province of China, as well as a national government. In practice, the provincial level had many parallel functions. The KMT were a minority of the population of an island that had been under Japanese occupation and set about establishing its authority in a variety of ways.

In the early days it operated partly through repression. After an uprising against the occupation, the indigenous population was kept under control through imprisonment and execution. Since then, a major political issue has been the battle between the 'mainlanders' and the indigenous population.

The other connected issue is that of the nature of Taiwan as an entity. Some believed it should strive to be independent, others that it is a province of China and its government should continue to claim to be the legitimate government of all of China, and still others who think it should be reunified with China and become a province of the PRC.

The balance of social forces in Taiwan has been largely determined by the development of the economy which in turn was dominated by KMT policy.[12] The first phase of development (about 1949–53) concentrated on land reform which displaced the rural landlords and created some support for the KMT among the farmers. Many of the displaced landlords developed into the first indigenous bourgeoisie.

The second phase of development (1953–6) was one of import substitution, in which the party-state developed industries, either directly or through the newly developed local business class. The ruling KMT was not dependent on the private sector for support or for the success of economic development, since they had aid and loan support from the USA, anxious to keep Taiwan as part of the capitalist world. What support it did need from the newly developing class of business people was gained by a system of 'clientilism'.[13] Since the party-state had control over credit, licences, and other essentials for business, support could be bought. The party at local level developed networks of support and control and the networks were enhanced by the local electoral system.

As the strategy developed towards one of export-oriented investment, the local business class grew in number and in wealth. Some of the old indigenous families were kept within the fold through benefiting from, for example, shares in state industries which were privatized.[14] Throughout the 1960s and 1970s the main political task was to prevent the social forces which were produced by economic growth from destroying the KMT hegemony. A major way in which the newly emerging middle class was incorporated was by maintaining the 'clientilist'[15] networks, sponsoring local business associations which were dependent on the state, and encouraging those with political ambitions to join the KMT. For example, the native Taiwanese membership of the KMT central committee grew from 6.1 per cent at the time of the tenth Party Congress (1969–76) to 19.3 per cent during the twelfth (1981–8).[16] Appointments to the civil service were also gradually opened up to native Taiwanese. Similar strategies were tried with the emerging trade union movement. State-sponsored unions were set up to make sure that the party kept control of most of the labour organizations.

These strategies were sufficient to stay in control until the end of the 1970s. There was a growing body of people, middle class, and working class, and some of those educated overseas who formed opposition to the KMT. There were two main issues. State domination of economic development restricted the chances of getting rich of those who were not part of the clientilist networks. The other was the Taiwanese nationalism of those who resented being dominated by the 'mainlanders' and those who wanted Taiwan to be an independent state. Later, there was a growing group of big business people trading with and investing in China, who wanted a more open policy of engagement with (the rest of) China through which they could pursue their business interests.

After the Kaoshiung incident of 1979, in which protesters were shot, organized opposition developed, represented by independent politicians who were not KMT members. By the early 1980s they were winning 20–30 per cent of the popular vote in local elections. The party-state came under pressure to liberalize and democratize. At this point the legislature was still occupied by those who had been elected in 1947. Chiang Ching-kuo, son[17] of and successor to Chiang Kai-shek, accepted that there were forces outside the party that needed to be accommodated if the party was to stay in control. In 1986, the ban on opposition parties was lifted and in 1987 martial law was officially ended. Many political parties were formed, but eventually the Democratic Progressive Party, which was formed in 1986 became the main opposition to the KMT, together with the New Party, formed in 1993 by dissident KMT members. In 1991 the old brigade of legislative assembly members were persuaded to retire and elections were held in late 1991. The KMT won 101 seats, the DPP 51, and independents 9.

After Chiang Ching-kuo's death in 1988, Lee Teng-hui became president, the first native Taiwanese to do so. Eventually a presidential election was held in 1996 and Lee was elected with 54 per cent of the vote. In the legislature election in 1995 and the national assembly election in 1996, the KMT won 46 and 49.7 per cent of the votes, respectively.

This progress towards democracy seems to support the thesis of the 'economic growth brings liberal democracy' school. A once dominant party, with no national elections, gave way to demands for freedom of association and free elections. As Lo put it: 'Democratization in Taiwan could be seen as a petty bourgeois revolution that eventually transformed the entire party-state.'[18]

While the elections to the presidency and the legislative yuan are now contested by genuinely free opposition parties, the KMT is still a very rich and powerful organization. It is also not above using its connections with criminal organizations to stay in power at local and national levels. According to Chu: 'politicians linked to criminal groups infest representative bodies at the county and township levels. The legislative yuan is an arena of horse-trading among state officials, party officials, and lawmakers acting as proxies for local factions and big businesses.'[19]

The connections between politics and organized crime became an issue in the 1996 presidential election. The Minister of Justice, Liao Cheng-hau claimed that about one-third of the county councillors and 5–10 per cent of the legislature and National Assembly had criminal records or strong connections with organized crime.[20] Justice Minister Ma Ying-jeou started prosecutions against 341 officials, none of whom was convicted. He was removed from office by the president, it is alleged, because of his excessive zeal in pursuing organized crime.[21]

The KMT took action to restore popular support in the face of these allegations and of widespread concern about the government's apparent inability to deal with organized crime, including kidnapping and murder of prominent people. Its weakening position in the National Assembly caused it to take action to correct its image of bribery, connections with organized crime, money-laundering, and the rest of the inheritance from a long period of one-party rule. It has arrested public figures who are suspected of having committed fraud and being members or leaders of triad societies. However, at the same time it appointed as chairman of the legislature's judiciary committee Luo Fu-tsu, known to be the leader of a prominent Taiwan gang.[22]

What seems to have happened is that there has developed a sufficiently strong opposition to the ruling KMT for the party to give in to pressure for elections and the development of independent parties and other organizations. Like any other political party, it wants to stay in power, and the habits of network development, vote buying, and other means of maintaining support die hard.

Korea

Korea was ruled by a military dictatorship from the military coup led by Park Chung Hee in 1961 until the elections for president in December 1987 and for the national assembly in April 1988. During that dictatorship political opposition was suppressed and after the transition to a form of democracy considerable liberalization took place. In response to demonstrations in June 1987 protesting at Roh Tae Woo's candidature for the presidency, a democratization programme was announced in what became known as the 29 June Statement. The national assembly was made more important and other changes were made to make the system more democratic, including respect for human rights, release of political prisoners, a free press, protection from interference for political parties, and restoration of local elections (in 1991). Legally, then, Korea is a democracy with direct elections to local and national assemblies and a directly elected president.

We saw in Chapter 3 that the big business empires in Korea were built by a coalition of business, government, and the military that was so close that the distinctions between the categories was unclear and that families and networks connected the groups together. This ruling élite has built Korea from a poverty-stricken derelict condition at the end of the Korean War to the world's fourteenth largest economy.

How did they stay in power? One of the main sources of opposition in Korea has been the labour movement. The main source of Korea's growth was the long hours, hard work, and low pay of the Korean industrial working class. They have not willingly accepted their role as uncomplaining wealth creators. Korean students and workers have accepted great risks by taking to the streets in demonstrations and organizing strikes in the face of well-organized and ruthless forces. On 26 December 1996, at 6 a.m. legal amendments were passed by the New Korea Party (the president's party) seriously reducing workers' rights. The strikes and demonstrations which followed involved 1 million trade unionists.[23] Korean Confederation of Trade Unions leaders and others were arrested, street battles ensued, and the strike cost over $3 billion in lost production. This is not to say that Korea does not have democratic features, but the combination of early-morning law-making and the response from organized workers shows that crucial political decisions are not always made using them. It also shows that changing the law to weaken trade union power and lower employers' costs are more important to the government than abstract notions of liberal democracy. The protests and riots continued. In June 1997, students clashed with riot police over Kim Young Sams's refusal to disclose his election campaign spending in the 1992 election campaign, for example.

Korean governments combine coercion with other strategies. The regular appearance of riot police in Seoul and other cities intimidates the diverse opposition as well as maintaining 'law and order'. There is a history of the use of the police in labour disputes. Ogle[24] documents the quasi-military nature of police involvement in putting down strikes in the late 1980s. One example was the attack in March 1989 on the Hyundai plant by 10,000 police. Ogle shows that there is close cooperation between the police and company management in the suppression of strikes and attempted squashing of trade union organization.

Kim Dae Jung was elected president at the end of 1997 and took up office in January 1998. He had been a member of the opposition who had been subject to severe repression by the government, including a kidnapping in 1973. He came to power on a platform of reducing the power of the *chaebol* and proceeded to put through measures to reduce their support and immunity from scrutiny. To consolidate his power he first ensured that his ministers were drawn largely from his home province. He avoided alienating even those previous presidents who had been imprisoned for corruption and murder. He then sought to establish control over the legislature by encouraging members to switch membership to his party (see Box 5.1).

Malaysia

Observers of Malaysian politics have invented special terms to describe the strategy of the government and the ruling party because standard terms seem not to apply there. Jesudason[25] has described it as a 'syncretic' state in which diverse elements are held together by a variety of oppressive and demagogic methods. Crouch[26] has compared Malaysia with the Netherlands, in that the state has to hold together (or sometimes keep apart) different ethnic and religious groups, and refers to a 'consociational' arrangement. He also describes the government's use of coercion when necessary as 'incremental authoritarianism'. Anne

Box 5.1 South Korea: Heads of Local Governments Rush to Defect to Ruling Camp for Self-Protection

Many newly elected heads of local government bodies are rushing to defect to the ruling camp after deserting the opposition Grand National Party, betraying citizens who voted for them in last month's local elections. In what appears to be a betrayal of their responsibility to work closely with the central government on behalf of the public in their region, 15 per cent of the mayors and county chiefs of the opposition camp defected to the ruling coalition. The ruling National Congress for New Politics (NCNP) received four of them this week in what it called a voluntary change of party affiliation. Nevertheless, there is no one in the current political circle who believes the four made their decisions of their own volition, political observers argued. Even those who defected to the ruling camp will admit privately that pressure was exerted on them by the present administration. The mayor of the city of Tonghae said at NCNP headquarters in Yoido Monday that he had made up his mind to join the NCNP in order to secure more budget funds from the central government. 'This was the most difficult decision of my entire career. I thought this would be the best for the people who voted for me. By joining the NCNP-ULD coalition I will certainly be able to obtain a bigger budget for my people,' said Kim In Ki, former member of the opposition GNP. Another member of the majority opposition party, waiting to join the NCNP following his departure from the party last week, said that he will be able to contribute to the development of the region he represents far more efficiently as a ruling party representative. 'After carefully considering the interests of the people in my region, I will soon join the rival party. All I am concerned about is how best to help the ones who supported me in the election,' said a local district head in Kyongsang-pukto. The secretary-general of the NCNP used similar logic during a reception to welcome new party members from the opposition. 'They made courageous resolutions to serve the nation and its people. I praise their intention. Together, we will reform the nation and promote a brighter future for future generations,' said Rep. Chung Kyun Hwan. In private conversation, however, they express different views, often severely criticizing the ruling party's strategies. 'I have seen my colleagues being threatened with prosecution every day since the local elections. All of us must surely have committed some errors in the past, including myself. To be honest, I am apprehensive about my future, assuming that I remain on the opposition side,' said a local government chief and member of the GNP. 'Even the ones who are proved to be innocent after a prosecutor's investigation will lose the faith of the public in the process. Their political careers will end for only being accused of bribery, regardless of the final verdicts,' he continued. The ruling camp put heavy pressure on the heads of local autonomous bodies which are affiliated with the opposition, together with prosecutors, in a bid to manipulate the political structure as part of the realignment process, according to a mayor in the capital region. So far eleven mayors and regional heads, out of the total of seventy-four who ran in the elections as GNP candidates have defected to the ruling coalition. 'If this is a case, the ruling party contenders may not even have to compete with opposition candidates in the race. The NCNP-ULD coalition can just wait until the elections are over and force opposition winners to give up their party affiliations. It will save them time and effort,' a political observer said, in reference to the NCNP's tactics.

Korea Times, 28 July 1998

Munro-Kua's expression 'authoritarian populist', combines repression with nationalism and leadership personality cults. Others have called the government 'soft authoritarian' which implies that intolerance of opposition does not extend to armed intervention.

New terms have been invented to describe the Malaysian situation because it seems not to conform to stereotypes either of democracy or authoritarian rule. Malaysia has elections, opposition parties, splits in the ruling party, different parties in power in the national government and some of the state governments, all of which make it look like a democracy. On the other hand, there have been strong emergency powers, arrest and imprisonment of politicians and trade unionist and student activists, a ban on students joining political parties without permission, all of which make the regime look like a dictatorship. The arrest of the deputy Prime Minister Anwar Ibrahim in September 1998 on charges of sexual misconduct and corruption may indicate a willingness to take politics outside the political arena, a willingness not confined to Malaysia.

There are also visible signs of old-fashioned corruption. A local change in party control can impoverish one set of families and enrich another overnight. The ruling party United Malays National Organization (UMNO) owns companies which have been given big government contracts, such as the construction of the north–south highway.

Its president for many years, Mahatir Mohamad, generated loyalty and affection among many at home and frequently fierce criticism abroad. During the Asian currencies crisis of 1997 a monosyllabic public row broke out in which George Soros, the currency speculator, attacked Mahatir's call for control of speculators and his undemocratic ways, while Mahatir condemned those who get rich from speculation at the expense of those who are trying to build nations on fast economic growth.

However hard it may be to find neat categories with which to explain Malaysian politics, we saw in Chapter 3 that governments have been successful, in the sense of generating economic growth and improving most of the population's living standards. UMNO and its coalition partners in the Barisa Nasional has maintained popular support, by whatever means, and has increased its support and the personal ratings of Mahatir, even among Malaysians of Chinese origin.[27] How have they done it?

Since independence in 1957 a major element of Malaysian politics has been the attempt by the ethnic majority to gain and maintain economic and political superiority over the other ethnic groups, especially people of Chinese origin who had tended to dominate most aspects of business, along with the colonial power. Malaysians of Malay origin (the 'Bumiputra') have dominated government and used their position to promote their interests. Positive discrimination has included a quota system in the universities, preferential treatment in business finance, differential access to housing loans, all in the interests of 'correcting imbalances' between the Bumiputra and the Chinese. Naturally, such munificence creates political support.

The second tactic of the ruling party has been the occasional use of force and repression to stifle opposition. The laws allowing draconian measures date from the colonial emergency proclamation of 1948, which gave the government powers of arrest and detention without trial in the interests of national security. These powers were replaced by the internal Security Act of 1960, augmented by the Essential (Security Cases) Regulations in 1975, a Sedition Act, an Official Secrets Act, and a Printing Presses Act to control the press. While these powers are often held in reserve by many states, in Malaysia they have been used fairly frequently to deal with political opposition as well as cases of threat to the existence of the state. While the states of emergency in 1964 (in response to Indonesia's declaration of territorial claims) and 1969 (after the 'race riots') may have been justified as cases of 'national security', the emergencies in Sarawak (1966) and Kelantan (1977) were more a threat to the ruling party than to the security of the state. The powers were used in the 1970s against opposition parties, trade unions, students, and even Christians accused of attempting to convert Muslims, all in the interests of national security.[28] Another tactic has been the use of money in politics, both of the 'pork barrel' type of siting projects in marginal constituencies and the purchase of votes. There has also been clientilism, similar to that in Taiwan, through which interests have been aligned through contracts and licences.

None of these tactics was unique to Malaysia. What is slightly special about Malaysia is the creative use of nationalism and nation-building along with economic development and the creation of a Malay capitalist class. In a sense, Mahatir's strategy looked towards Japan: the merging of self-interest and national interest, strong ties between business, politics, and the bureaucracy, and politics based more on factional and geographical interests than on parties representing class groupings. Of course, Malaysia's ethnic diversity and regional economic differences between peninsular Malaysia and Sabah and Sarawak made the creation of national unity much harder than in Japan's case.

Indonesia

Few democratic institutions existed in Indonesia before the general election of 1999. The president was chosen by the People's Consultative Assembly more than half of whose members were chosen by the president. The military was formally represented in the Assembly and informally very close to the government whose president for more than three decades, President Suharto, was himself an army general. There was no independent judiciary; political detainees could disappear without trial. The killings following the failed coup in 1965/6 were directed towards suspected communists and especially towards Chinese Indonesians. The invasion of East Timor in 1975 and the subsequent killings were indicative of the regime's style. Dissent was not tolerated and newspapers that published disagreement were closed.

The USA and international organizations mainly supported this style of government. From 1967 there was a steady flow of foreign aid and loans, organized through the Inter-Governmental Group on Indonesia. The Clinton government had a brief period of objecting to the government's human rights record but dropped its objections when it decided to decouple trade and human rights in its relationship with China.

As well as these repressive measures, the Suharto government also stifled or incorporated opposition forces. The ruling party, Golkar, was naturally backed by the military but the government also funded approved opposition parties and business and youth organizations that might otherwise have developed views in opposition to the government.[29]

The 'New Order' government maintained the support of business through its patronage networks. Even the period of economic liberalization was managed in favour of the existing powerful business groups. Vatikiotis[30] has shown that even when trade was liberalized, the old monopolies were consulted and were able to take advantage of the new rules. New Order supporters were able to benefit from all the economic policies, including the promotion of non-oil exports.

As well as patronage through government contracts and licences, Suharto used a peculiarly Indonesian institution to maintain his networks. The Dutch had created a form of charitable fund (called 'yayasan') which was untaxed and unaccountable and formed a useful vehicle to store and pay out cash for worthy causes and to buy support. The vehicle was used by many very rich individuals and corporations.

Indonesia was the country in the region singled out for criticism of 'cronyism' and the lack of liberal economics. Nobody could do business without some sort of connection, bribery was normal, and government revenues and private funds were often indistinguishable. Growth, while fast enough to keep the government in power, could have been better. Deforestation of Kalimantan could have been controlled. The country could have been less dependent on oil revenues which still accounted for 39 per cent of foreign exchange earnings in 1990.

Some commentators have hailed the replacement of Suharto by B. J. Habibie as a sign of the replacement of the New Order by a new regime. The resignation of Suharto after the student and worker demonstrations in 1998 looked as if it might represent the victory of the people over the military-backed government. In a sense it did, but the events were the culmination of a longer process.

Habibie was already an important figure in the Suharto government. In 1990 he had been appointed by Suharto as head of the Muslim Intellectual Organization in an effort to maintain Muslim support for the government. One interpretation of the tactic was that it was part of Suharto's strategy of try-ing to represent the balance of forces between the old Java élite, including the army, and the class of Muslim business people and intellectuals. While Habibie was an outsider as far as the army was concerned he was part of Suharto's strategy. His eventual choice as president represents the reality of the need to incorporate these groups. Habibie was in any case a part of the network of government and business contacts and a beneficiary of it, in his role as owner of various engineering businesses. He had started the process of talking to dissidents and opening up the government to a wider range of inter-ests as early as 1992.

It is possible that 1998 was a watershed in Indonesian politics. The combina-tion of the end of Suharto's long period of rule and the economic collapse may have damaged for ever the network of business, military, and government contacts which has run the country since at least 1966. Certainly there has been a flowering of dozens of new political parties wanting to contest the 1999 general election. Some of the parties, such as the Justice Party, arose from the student demonstrations. At the announcement of the formation of one of the new parties, the People's Sovereignty Party, in August 1998 R. O. Tambunan said: 'Over the thirty-two years of New Order rule, political parties did not function as a channel for the people's aspirations; rather they served merely as tools to perpetuate the power of Soeharto's regime.'[31] It remains to be seen whether the regime has finished or whether it has been simply handed over to a new set of guardians.

Philippines

The Philippines had a long history of democratic elections from 1907 during the period of US colonization. From independence from the USA in 1945 until 1972 it was run as a democracy. President Marcos was elected in 1965 and declared martial law in 1972. Marcos wrote a new constitution that gave the president control over all parts of the state. While a National Assembly was established in 1978, an amendment gave the president all law-making powers.

The Marcos regime was an example of an alliance of élite forces and the mili-tary using the apparatus of government to make themselves rich. Monopolies and oligopolies were established in lucrative sectors, including sugar, coconuts, construction, gambling, and insurance. Marcos and his family amassed fortunes, much of it deposited overseas. When the regime was replaced, the new government estimated that $5 billion had been hidden away.

Nor was the government an economic success. It set up some of the arrangements which other 'strong state' regimes had, including the National Economic Development Authority and a string of state-owned enterprises most of which made losses. Foreign investment was liberalized, as was foreign exchange borrowing (overseas debt grew from $2.2 billion at the start of the martial law period to $26.5 at the end). The programme was called 'Building a New Society'.

The period of martial law came to an end in 1986, when there were mass demonstrations. Marcos resigned and in the following elections Corazon Aquino, whose family had suffered at the hands of the Marcos regime, was elected president. She maintained constitutional democracy, holding elections in 1987, 1988, and 1992. She attempted to break up the Marcos networks, including the agricultural monopolies, liberalized trade and investment, and privatized most of the state enterprises. She lost the 1992 election and was replaced by Fidel Ramos, who had been chief of police under Marcos. Ramos continued the process of liberalization but his government was still one of cronyism and special privileges. He did, however, open up the processes of government to a wider range of forces and made alliances with opposition political parties.

Ramos's term of office expired in 1998 and he was persuaded (partly by popular demonstrations) not to extend his period of office. He was replaced by Joseph Estrada who became president at the end of June 1998. Estrada presented himself as a reluctant president who would rather have stayed in his previous career as film star, even though he had been a close ally of Ramos and had been appointed vice-president in 1992. Estrada made an arrangement with Imelda Marcos by which some of the family's frozen fortune could be released and freed some of the sequestered assets of Marcos's associates[32]. He also appointed Marcos people to some of the most important positions in government.

The long period of democracy had managed to incorporate members of the growing middle classes into supporting the government but it had not removed the hold of the hundred or so families who run most of the country and own a large proportion of the land. The Philippines was never one of the fastest-growing economies of the region, despite the trappings of a developmental state and despite an authoritarian regime.

ASIAN DEMOCRACY?

These vignettes of politics and the economy in a sample of countries show that there is a wide variety of political institutions and practices. The military influence varies, as does the way in which élites react to the development of new classes.

Can we see any patterns of similarity in the politics and the relationships between politics and the economies? If there are similarities, this does not imply that the similarities also represent a difference from some stereotype of Western democracy. The West also has a variety of practices. The lobbying and funding system which guarantees corporations' access to legislators in the USA is not fundamentally different from the close relationships between government and business in a variety of Asian states.

Patronage and clientilism

Elections do not change the nature of the connections between parties, governments, and businesses. They may change the personnel involved in the networks, especially on the government side, but they do not necessarily change the organizational boundaries. In Korea, in which a previous radical and dissident, Kim Dae Jung, was elected, attempts to change the system of government backing for business were very hard to implement and much of the legislation was bogged down in the parliamentary process. Similarly in Japan changes to the financial system and the relationships between businesses and the state were hard to change. In other cases, such as the Philippines and Indonesia, the post-crisis elections mainly change the cast in the drama rather than the script.

Clientilism, the use of exchanges of economic opportunities for political support, operates through a network of connections. The networks can adapt and grow to incorporate new members whose economic positions improve with economic development. Networks based on old economic power, especially derived from landownership and agriculture are unlikely to be extensive enough to resist being replaced. One of the reasons for the difficulty the Japanese political élite had in turning around the country's economic difficulties is that the government was too dependent on the farmers and support from the rural areas to make policies which ignored their interests. Reflation through public spending was centred on construction and public works projects which would gain support from their mainly rural beneficiaries but lose the support of their mainly urban taxpaying funders.

The replacement of a president or a ruling party does not change the power relations on which networks are based although they may adjust the membership of the networks. The advantage of democracy is that it allows adjustment in the ruling networks to take account of new economic forces in the management of the country. Where there are no elections, as in China, the adjustment of networks takes place through other means. Politics within the party can generate new alliances and allow new social forces, such as politicians representing newly rich provinces or cities, to join decision-making processes of governments.

Parties and representation

Political parties do not necessarily represent nationwide interests such as those of manufacturing owners, workers, or farmers. Parties are just as likely to represent local interests or to be simply a grouping with a source of political support rather than an identifiable economic interest. The flowering of parties in Indonesia for the 1999 elections does not reflect the forces operating in the country. Some parties do, such as those representing strands of Islam or approaches to the democratic process, but others are simply competitive blocs.

If the prize from political success is a place in a patronage network for the winners, the main tactic of politics will simply be gaining enough support to take that place. There are exceptions. The KMT was initially successful as a hegemonic, foreign force. Once the economic development generated new and sometimes indigenous economic groups, some thought it best to represent themselves outside the KMT.

There are few examples of parties representing worker interests. If there were communist parties which might have taken on this role, as in Malaysia, the Philippines, and Indonesia they were successfully suppressed. Where they survived, as in Japan, they have decreased in importance.

The party-state

In some cases the boundary between the ruling party and the state is very blurred. Long periods of one-party domination in Singapore, China, and until the late 1980s in Japan blended the processes of government with the processes of intraparty politics. Power relationships can only be understood as operating in parallel organizations. The party secretary who is also the general manager of the state-owned enterprise will have a different relationship with the local branch of the bank than will the general manager who is not the party secretary. What is special about the party-state is that there is hardly a boundary between the two institutions. Democratic processes to gain office in the state do not necessarily have their parallels inside the party system. Patronage, nepotism, and expressive networks can all take place within the party and spill over into the state apparatus.

It is unlikely that the Asian states are developing towards either a European or North American model of democracy. There are many deep-rooted features of all the societies which will most likely result in their own trajectories. Even the proponent of convergence on liberal democracy, Frances Fukuyama, concedes:

On the other hand, virtually no one in Asia today believes it likely that Asian societies will ultimately converge with the particular model of liberal democracy represented by the contemporary United States, or, indeed, that such a state of affairs is remotely desirable. If Asia's Confucian traditions allow it to find an appropriate and stable balance between the need for liberty and the need for community, in the end it will be a politically happy place indeed.[33]

Where democratic institutions have been established and free elections held there have certainly been challenges to ruling parties and to the élites they represent, especially in the relatively recently established democracies of Taiwan and Korea. The response has been to strengthen practices of patronage and clientilism and other means of gaining and retaining power. As to the supposed Confucian abhorrence of confrontation and competition in the political arena, it is difficult to see where this occurs. National assemblies in various countries in the region are far from calm and harmonious and political demonstrations and governments' responses to them hardly suggest an unwillingness to disagree in public. The arguments against confrontational elections were mainly made by those in the dominant parties that they wanted to keep dominant.

Can it be said that there is a special 'Asian' form of politics emerging in the region? The answer to this question depends on whether the practices in the region differ systematically from practices elsewhere. The use of networks of personal connections, the use of government contracts to pay political debts, vote influencing by the siting of developments, and infrastructure improvements are by no means exclusive to the region.

NOTES

1. J. F. Helliwell, 'Empirical Linkages between Democracy and Economic Growth', *British Journal of Political Science*, 24 (1994).
2. S. P. Huntington, *The Third Way: Democratization in the Late Twentieth Century* (Norman: University of Oklahoma Press, 1991).
3. F. Fukuyama, *Trust* (New York: Free Press, 1995).
4. Ibid. 4.
5. Ibid. 356.
6. Dr Mahatir Mohamad became prime minister of Malaysia in 1981.
7. James Chul-Yul Soong, 'Political Development in the Republic of China on Taiwan, 1985–92: An Insider's View', *World Affairs*, 155/2 (1992): 62.
8. See D. A. Bell, D. Brown, K. Hayasuriya, and D. M. Jones (eds.), *Towards Illiberal Democracy in Pacific Asia* (Basingstoke: Macmillan, 1995).
9. Reported in Taiwan's Central News Agency, 5 Dec. 1998.
10. This argument is based on H. Crouch, *The Asian Economic Crisis and Democracy* (Conference Paper, City University of Hong Kong, 1998).
11. See A. Munro-Kua, *Authoritarian Populism in Malaysia* (Basingstoke: Macmillan, 1996).
12. See Lo Shiu Hing, 'Liberalization and Democratization in Taiwan: A Class and Functional Perspective', in A. Laothamatas (ed.), *Democratization in Southeast and East Asia* (New York: St Martin's Press, 1997).

13. See F. Wang, 'The Political Economy of Authoritarian Clientilism in Taiwan', in L. Roniger and G. Ayşe (eds.), *Democracy, Clientilism and Civil Society* (Boulder, Colo.: Lynne Rienner, 1994).

14. Ibid.

15. 'Clientilism' is the use of favours to create and maintain political support.

16. Chu Yun-han, 'Taiwan's Unique Challenges, *Journal of Democracy*, 7/3 (1996) and S. Rigger, 'Taiwan: Mobilisational Authoritarianism', in G. Rodan (ed.), *Political Oppositions in Industrialising Asia* (London: Routledge, 1996).

17. While there have been controversial reports in Taiwan that he was not the biological son of Chiang Kai-shek, he was his successor..

18. Lo Shiu-hing, 'Liberalization and Democratization in Taiwan': 225.

19. Chu Yun-han, 'Taiwan's Unique Challenges':77.

20. Cheng Tun-jen, 'Taiwan in 1996—From Euphoria to Melodrama', *Asian Survey* 37/1 (1997).

21. Shaw Sing-ning, 'A Dissenting Voice—Dealing with the Godfather', *Asia Inc*, May 1997.

22. *Far East Economic Review*, 1 May 1997.

23. C. Jay Ou, *Multinational Monitor*, 18/3 (1997).

24. G. E. Ogle, *South Korea: Dissent within the Economic Miracle* (London: Zed Books, 1990).

25. J. V. Jesudason, 'Malaysia: the Syncretic State', in G. Rodan (ed.), *Political Oppositions in Industrialising Asia* (London: Routledge, 1996).

26. H. Crouch, *Government and Society in Malaysia* (Ithaca: Cornell University Press, 1996).

27. For a detailed report on the 1995 general elections see E. T. Gomez, *The 1995 Malaysian General Elections* (Singapore: Institute of Southeast Asian Studies, Occasional Paper 93, 1996).

28. For details see ch. 6 of A. Munro-Kua, *Authoritarian Populism in Malaysia.*

29. See A. Santoso, 'Democratization: The Case of Indonesia's New Order' in A. Laothamatas (ed.), *Democratization in Southeast and East Asia* (New York: St Martin's Press, 1997).

30. M. R. J. Vatikiotis, *Indonesian Politics Under Suharto* (London: Routledge, 1994): 44–5.

31. *Jakarta Post*, 10 Aug. 1998.

32. *Gulf News*, 17 July 1998.

33. F. Fukuyama, 'Confucianism and Democracy', *Journal of Democracy*, 6/2 (1995): 33.

6

The Family, the Company, and the State

This chapter puts the question: how do people in the region make provision for old age and periods of sickness and unemployment? This includes the question of how generations look after each other, how much people save, and what role governments play in this area. These questions are related to economic development in two ways: the savings rate of some countries has been high and the savings of individuals and families have been made available, through the banks, for investment. The degree to which the state is involved in collecting savings through taxation and how the state uses those savings has also had an impact on government investment and on the level of taxation.

It shows that while there are some common features among the countries, there is also a wide variety of arrangements. Some academics have argued that in the north of the region there is an 'East Asian welfare model',[1] based on individual and family responsibility, collective responsibilities organized through some sort of insurance, and a level of state responsibility that is lower than that generally accepted in Europe. While a 'model' may be discernible and there are levels of state involvement which are low compared with most of Europe and Australasia, there is also a great variety. Japan, Korea, and Taiwan have developed insurance systems and Singapore has, through the Central Provident Fund, a high level of enforced saving for old age, amounting to a 'tax' of 40 per cent of incomes. Hong Kong has a minimal level of state involvement and has just introduced a provident fund far less inclusive than Singapore's. In China, the party-state has, since the revolution, taken care of state workers' welfare, largely left the peasants to fend for themselves, and is now going through a period of reducing state enterprises' responsibilities for their workers. In the south of the region there is less state involvement in people's lives as far as old age and sickness is concerned.

RIGHTS AND OBLIGATIONS

Family

Attitudes of generations to each other in families are one of the main determinants of how people make provision for their old age. One of the central tenets of Confucianism is that everyone's position in the family in relation to the other family members brings with it certain obligations. Such a notion is of course not exclusive to Confucianism and can be found in Islam, Judaism, Hinduism, and other religions. If family obligations, especially of children to their parents, remain strong, it can have a big impact on the welfare of people as they age. If such obligations break down, the opposite effect takes hold.

There are three reasons why such intergenerational obligations might break down. First is the simple capacity of one generation to look after its elders: if family size shrinks there may simply not be enough money for the one or two surviving children to afford to look after their parents. This may be especially difficult if at the same time people live for much longer. The prospect of one surviving 70+-year-old looking after her 90+-year-old parents is less likely than a 30+ looking after parents whose life expectancy is in the fifties. Economic growth has brought an increase in life expectancy which older attitudes to ageing might not be able to cope with. For example, life expectancy in China before the revolution was under 40 years and is now over 70 years.[2] Average life expectancy in Japan similarly went up from 58 in 1950 to 77 in 1995 for men and from 61 to 83 for women. More fundamentally, the wish to look after the elders may fade. Migration away from the family home, the establishment of an employment relationship, and a more instrumental attitude to life and obligations may leave older generations abandoned.

Selfishness and individualism can reduce the desire of one generation to look after another, but it does not have to. A survey of ageing in ASEAN in 1989 showed that older people (in this case defined as people aged 65+) were still predominantly living with other family members as well as their spouse and that very few people were living on their own. In Indonesia, Malaysia, Philippines, and Singapore only 8 per cent, 6.4 per cent, 3 per cent and 2.3 per cent of people lived alone and around 10 per cent lived with their spouse only.[3] In Japan, more older people lived alone and the proportion grew during the thirty years to 1990, as shown in Table 6.1

A sample survey of people aged 60+ in China in 1987 showed that at that point 50 per cent of old people lived in a three-generation family. In the urban areas, 70 per cent of the older people had pensions while in the countryside 67 per cent relied on their children and 20 per cent were still working. Only 7 per cent of the urban population were still working.[4] This survey showed the big difference between the welfare status of peasants and urban workers: the pensions provided by employers in the urban areas make for a secure if frugal old age while in the countryside the old people still relied mainly on their chil-

Table 6.1 Japan: population over 65 and their ways of living (% of total)

	1960	1990
Living with relatives	85	61
Living with spouse	8	22
Living alone	4	12
Other (institutions, etc.)	3	5

Source: Takahashi (1997: 227)

dren. It remains to be seen whether the one-child policy will destroy the ability of future generations to take care of their elderly parents. The uncertainty in the urban areas arises from the serious problems of profitability and survival that the state-owned enterprises are facing. They constitute a rapidly shrinking proportion of the employment in the urban areas and many are unable to meet their social obligations. Soon there will be a generation of SOE employees whose pensions will no longer be guaranteed by their employers and whose families will not have been expecting to be looked after in old age.

While the increase in life expectancy and a growing demographic imbalance between workers and dependants can generate a society in which older people are uncared for, it does not follow that governments will do something to solve the problem. While the fact of having a small number of children clearly reduces the capacity of a generation to look after its parents, there is evidence that extended families can survive migration and, no longer sharing space, still support themselves.

In some cases the obligation to look after parents is reinforced by law. In Japan, the eldest son was, until 1948, obliged to take care of his parents. After 1948 this obligation was transferred to the whole of the immediate family. In Singapore the Maintenance of Parents Act empowers parents to take legal action against their children if they do not fulfil their obligations. Similar laws are in place in Taiwan and the PRC.

Companies

The right (and obligation) to work if physically able is an important principle which was easily upheld during the period of rapid economic growth. In Japan, companies accepted the responsibility to set up businesses to absorb workers who were surplus to requirements.[5] In China the SOEs were obliged to continue to employ workers who were surplus to requirements and indeed to accept workers posted to them by the party, whether they were required or not. While no such obligations have been accepted by firms in Hong Kong and Singapore, migration to both places has been controlled to make sure that there is rarely a surplus of labour.

In China and Japan the workplace became more than a place to earn wages. In the state-owned enterprises in China, the company (*danwei*) was responsible for its workers' housing, children's education, healthcare, and provisions for retirement. In larger companies in Japan, the company also took responsibility for paying retirement allowances and for other welfare schemes as well as legislated welfare contributions. In companies employing more than 5,000 people, 19 per cent of total labour costs are spent on these provisions, while the small firms paid 15 per cent.[6] While these are small proportions by European standards, they show that collective provision for these matters is centred on the workplace rather than the state at national or local level. In the case of the PRC, of course, it is difficult to distinguish the enterprise from the state and from the party as was clear in Chapter 3.

But, in both countries, for those workers who are attached to such an enterprise the ties between the worker and the workplace were far greater than the employment relationship. The workers offer loyalty and subjection to a high degree of socialization and/or social control in exchange for a job for life. Social contacts and social status come from membership of the workplace, which in itself will be linked to family as jobs are handed from generation to generation and recruitment is done by word of mouth through family networks.

In both cases, these close ties are under pressure. In Japan, the position of women, implied by the company employing the men and paying family allowances to support children, is becoming less acceptable and fewer women are willing to be a 'housewife'. Takahashi [7] shows that married women made up 58 per cent of working women in 1990, compared with 24 per cent in 1960 and that the average age of working women went up from 26 to 36 over the same period.[8]

The second pressure is from the effects of competition on the labour market. While protected industries could organize themselves by hiring workers for life and paying for loyalty with benefits in addition to wages, cost competition from firms with low-wage strategies makes this more difficult. In China, the growth of competition from private and township and village enterprises made it more difficult for state enterprises to afford their social obligations. In Japan, openness to international competition had some of the same effects. In Korea, the *chaebol* had a less interlocking relationship with employees but were, until changes in labour laws in 1997, legally obliged to offer job protection, under the Labour Standards Law of 1984.

In the rest of the region, such company-as-family relationships were not common. In Taiwan, the smaller companies and in Hong Kong some large ones were not company-as-family, rather family-as-company. However, in these cases the protection and benefits offered by the company would be differentiated between real members of the family and employees.

Such ties between workers and employers are not limited to Asia: the burden of health insurance contributions for businesses in the USA was one reason for the reform of the healthcare system there and there are still companies in Europe that operate a policy of worker loyalty through work guarantee.

Savings and self-reliance

An important element in the economic growth of the region was the ability to mobilize personal savings. Savings rates of 30 per cent or more were made available for investment through the banking system and provided bank liquidity and therefore credit to companies in the fast expansion period.

In Singapore, and in Korea after 1988, savings were compulsorily contributed to the provident fund. The government can use the fund for infrastructure or other projects (in Korea, over 50 per cent of the provident fund was borrowed by the government)[9] but individuals have a claim on their contributions. It is a hybrid between taxation and saving. It allows governments to raise funds without raising taxation and the possible resistance that might cause. In Japan central and especially local government achieved the same objectives by issuing bonds instead of raising taxes. High savings, if well invested, provide for secure old age. Savings ratios for a selection of countries in the region are shown in Table 6.2. Savings produce a virtuous circle, at least for a while (see Figure 6.1 'virtuous circle').

Table 6.2   Gross national savings as percentage of GNP, 1997

Hong Kong	33.7
Korea	34.7
Singapore	51.3
Taiwan	26.5
PRC	38.6
Indonesia	35.2
Malaysia	12.1 (1995)
Philippines	35.6

Source: Asian Development Bank, *Outlook 1997*: 229

The high savings rate has also been a main source of welfare as people made provision for their own and their preceding and succeeding generations' old age or periods of unemployment. These savings were an important element of the economic success of countries with high savings ratios. It could be argued that the attitude of self-reliance and savings provided the capital for the investment that generated the economic success. But they also produce vulnerability if dissaving starts because of ageing.[10] As old people use up their savings, bank liquidity suffers and corporations have to borrow from foreigners at higher rates and under different rules, losing control of their investments. This did not happen in the recent crisis in Japan as savings rates have not yet declined because of demographic effects but as the ageing process continues it may happen soon.

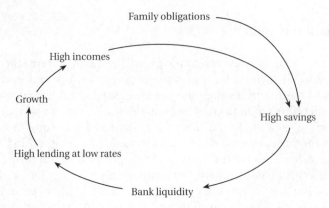

FIG. 6.1 **The 'virtuous circle'**

The state and welfare

One of the reasons for the big differences in state spending on welfare between Asia and Northern Europe is that even where there are schemes for wide or universal access to services or protection, that access is often arranged under state regulation or encouragement rather than through taxation and direct provision.

The idea that citizenship brings with it a right to a minimum standard of welfare which should be provided even when the citizen is unable to work, through age, misfortune, or disability is not a common one outside Europe. The existence of a right implies that someone else has an obligation. The idea that a state has an obligation to allow citizens a welfare right when they cannot provide for their own welfare implies that there is some sort of contract between the state and the citizens, which is also itself peculiar to a particular historical conjuncture.[11] The USA tried to impose a notion of welfare rights on Japan when the daily Life Security Law was introduced in Japan in 1946, changing the state's welfare obligation from one of 'mercy' to a 'right'.[12]

In none of the countries, until recent years, were there schemes of unemployment benefit provided by the state, though there have been unemployment insurance provisions. Because of this, 'unemployment' as measured also becomes a socially constructed and society-specific idea. In Hong Kong, for example, the alternative to a 'proper job' for many people is to become a street trader, whether legal and licensed or unlicensed. The number of street traders rises and falls with the employment cycle. No street trader is unemployed but they may be on very low income. If there were unemployment benefit at the same rate, they would be defined as unemployed. Similarly the workers still employed in SOEs in China which have ceased production may be unpaid by the work unit and doing other things to make a living but they are not officially unemployed. If there is no obligation to employ, there is no right to work. In no case has the state taken on a legal obligation to employ. If there is an obligation to work but no right to a job, people will find some way of making a living, find family support, or starve.

Where there are a large number of rural–urban migrants who still have a base in their rural land of origin, the obligation to work can be met by accepting a much-reduced standard of living in the countryside.

Even in those countries which have made state provision for welfare services and protection, the first priority has been economic development and any threat to development posed by disincentive effects of welfare provision or high taxes has been avoided. Goh Keng Swee, then Deputy Prime Minister of Singapore expressed a typical view of the dangers of a too generous welfare policy in 1976:

[N]othing is for free in this world and the end result of indiscriminate welfare state policies is bankruptcy. . . . In several West European countries, unemployment benefits have been so generous that some workers are better off unemployed! The money to pay for welfare state expenditure must come either from taxes or from the printing press.[13]

While Japan had a brief period during which a 'Japanese welfare model' was being developed, that was abandoned after the 1973 oil price rise and welfare was again subordinated to economic development in government priorities.

Japan

The origins of Japan's welfare system may be seen in the Allied occupation. Curiously the officers from the USA who designed the immediate post-war legislation had the idea that the state had an obligation to help people in their everyday lives. As Takahashi reports this did not necessarily coincide with what the US government thought or did at home:

[S]uch an idea that the state should guarantee the right to live a life in proper mode as a basic human right in democratic society was an idea of these American officers who were sent to Japan rather than the 'social policies' implemented in the United States in the late 1940s after the New Deal was over.[14]

In 1946 the Daily Life Security Law enacted the idea of equal rights rather than rights based on social status as had previously been the case. While the right did not extend to people classed as lazy or people who had relatives capable of looking after them, there was the basic idea that the state had a residual responsibility for individuals' welfare. The responsibility of the family was also redefined. In 1948 the Civil Code said that the whole family had a responsibility to look after old people, rather than the eldest son, as had been the case before the War. This law is frequently used to ensure that families do look after their older members.

The definition of a minimum standard to which people were entitled was the subject of contestation by the trade unions and the Communist Party. The conflict centred between 1957 and 1960 on a legal case about what constituted an acceptable standard of living and resulted in an 18 per cent increase in the income required to meet it. By 1961 there was universal coverage of medical insurance and pensions.

During the 1960s, Takahashi says, the migration of agricultural workers to the cities and the declining capacity of the family and people in local areas to care for all its members led to an increase in state welfare provision. Through the 1970s cuts in welfare expenditure would have been politically difficult and by the 1980s welfare spending was seen by many politicians as a burden and a hindrance to faster economic growth. The Liberal Democratic Party blamed the other parties at local level for the profligacy in welfare spending and loose fiscal regimes. The right wing started to campaign against the chance of Japan suffering from the 'British disease' and later the 'European disease'. All the problems of the West were seen as a package: stagnating economies, fiscal crises, strikes, unstable politics, and a lazy workforce feather-bedded by generous welfare provisions.

The government published the Life Cycle Plan in 1975 which set out a welfare model based on self-reliance and the family in explicit contrast to the West. The White Paper on Health and Welfare of 1978 contrasted the Japanese three-generation family with the atomized nuclear family of the West. Next year the LDP published its ideas about a Japanese model welfare society, about half of which consisted of an attack on the mistakes of the welfare systems in Britain and Sweden.

The problem of ageing population dominated the debate in the 1990s. Japan hit the problem of imbalance between working age and elderly population later than many Western countries. At the end of the 1980s the government had two responses, the 1988 welfare vision which advocated people working longer and the 1989 Gold Plan which contained a series of proposals for the integrated health and social care of very old people.

Meanwhile the large corporations had made their own welfare and insurance arrangements for their core employees, including family allowances, company pensions, housing allowances, and generous severance payments. While useful in developing loyalty, these programmes were expensive and affected these companies' competitiveness. Ito Peng calculated that non-wage labour costs in Japanese companies rose slowly from about 14 per cent of the total labour bill in 1975 to 17 per cent in 1995 (see Table 6.3). While apparently burdensome, these figures are much lower than the healthcare costs borne by companies in the USA over the same period (see Table 6.3). They did mean that for this sector of workers the state had only a small involvement in welfare programmes. It was only towards the end of the 1990s that the state became heavily involved in long-term care of the elderly, organizing home help services, day care, short-stay facilities, and other services which had previously been left to families, voluntary organizations, or local governments.[15]

Peng argues that Japanese corporations changed their hiring practices away from permanent employees and towards temporary workers towards the end of the 1990s to avoid the burden of these welfare arrangements, especially the

Table 6.3 Labour costs in Japan, 1975–1995 (yen/month and %)

	Total labour cost	Total wages	Other labour costs	Other costs % of total
1975	198,000	170,000	27,000	14
1985	362,000	306,000	56,000	15
1995	483,000	401,000	82,000	17

Source: Peng (1998: 28)

compulsory elements. The state was therefore under some pressure to find substitutes for the corporate schemes.

The other major issue is the result of the inability of the major corporations to continue to meet their welfare obligations. Presumably the government, in the current climate, will not willingly develop state-based welfare programmes to replace the company ones.

China

Some of China's welfare policy is similar to Japan's—there is a great reluctance to develop a 'welfare state'; companies (albeit state-owned) are the main source of welfare, including housing and pensions and healthcare, to a large proportion of core urban workers; companies' inability or unwillingness to continue in the role of 'looking after' workers is causing problems for workers and government.

Before the economic reforms initiated by Deng Xiao Ping in 1978, there was no official problem of unemployment in the urban areas: workers had a duty to work and the state-owned enterprises had a responsibility to employ them. Enterprises absorbed workers by reducing productivity. At the same time the enterprises had obligations to their employees, not just to pay salaries but to arrange housing, healthcare, education, and pensions. When enterprises were not in competition with each other or with foreign firms, the costs implied by low productivity (combined with low wages by international standards) and high social obligations were not a problem. The opening up of the economy to firms without such obligations (whether financed by internal or foreign funds) meant that the SOEs had to compete. Both employee numbers and the 'social wage' were a hindrance to competition. The SOEs were a major contributor to state funds, at all levels, while they made a profit. As competition reduced profitability, their contribution to state finance also reduced.

The government's response was a reform programme to restore profitability to the enterprises, or close them. The enterprises' response was to lay off workers in a search for productivity improvement. The result was a big increase in unemployment. By 1997, official estimates of unemployment in the urban areas were around 3 per cent, while unofficial estimates were twice this proportion. Workers' response has sometimes been public protest – an almost daily occurrence in China's 'rust belt' where obsolete industries are located. The party-state's response has been a mixture of measures to find jobs for the laid-off workers and various relief payments; for the longer term a national scheme for unemployment insurance, funded by contributions of 3 per cent of SOEs' and other enterprises' wage bills.[16]

Much of the initiative for both job-finding and unemployment pay came at local level, especially from Shanghai. The Shanghai approach involves an unemployment service centre signing a contract with an unemployed person under which it provides, for three years, living expenses, contributions to health and pension funds, training, and a job-finding service. Naturally such a contract is more easily delivered in a growing city such as Shanghai than in a province which is dominated by failing state-owned enterprises. In places where there is no growth the government is starting public works projects to boost the economy and employment. The main solution to the unemployment problem, according to the government, is economic growth. A growth target of 9 per cent per annum would stabilize unemployment. The crisis in the region makes such a growth rate unlikely.

Singapore

Singapore's politicians have been among the most vociferous in denouncing the idea of a welfare state, advocating hard work and self-reliance while building a society with more state involvement in welfare than any other in the region. The Housing Development Board established in 1960 built public housing to such an extent that 86 per cent of people in Singapore were living in public housing by 1996.[17] The CPF[18] (see Box 6.1), while not officially a tax-funded but a savings programme, effectively established a 40 per cent taxation regime out of which was financed retirement, health, housing, and a proxy unemployment insurance scheme.

The differences between Singapore and 'welfare states' are that the state mandated the CPF rather than collected taxes, that CPF only covers 70 per cent of the population, and that therefore the bottom 30 per cent of the workforce is not covered by any national social security or welfare programmes. As in Japan, the welfare regime is designed to underpin the labour market and to contribute to economic growth.

Korea

The military introduced some impressive social legislation in the 1960s[19] most of which was not implemented. Instead, the military governments introduced pensions and insurance plans for military and government personnel.

The only serious development of state-led protection came at the end of the

Box 6.1 The Central Provident Fund in Singapore

The CPF was started in 1954 as a save-as-you-earn fully funded retirement scheme. Many British colonies had a similar scheme and they spread to Taiwan and Indonesia in the early 1950s. Not all British colonies had a provident fund—some had social insurance schemes. Hong Kong had neither—rather a small, residual public assistance scheme and reliance on charities.

The CPF was developed into an important tool of social policy in health, education, and housing and as a source of funds for investment. Since 1994 the contribution rates have been 20 per cent each for employers and employees. Total membership (1995) at 2.7 million members covered 89.8 per cent of the resident population and active membership covered 70.6 per cent of the labour force. Individuals can draw on their savings for housing, health, and education expenditures as well as using them as a pension fund.

The Singapore scheme has benefited from certain elements that may not be available elsewhere. It was started early at a low level of contributions (5 per cent each for employee and employer) and was able to build up gradually to 20 per cent each. It has consistently had more people joining the scheme than withdrawing their funds at 55. It has been administered by a government which has been politically able to impose a mandatory contribution which might have been less easy elsewhere. Full employment in Singapore for almost the whole life of the scheme has made it well-funded.

The main drawback is the fact that it still leaves about 30 per cent of the workforce not covered.

1980s with a series of pension, medical insurance, and minimum wage measures all of which followed the major unrest of 1987–8. By the end of the 1990s 7.5 million people were covered by the national pension scheme (in addition to those covered under the government employee programme). An employment insurance system was introduced in 1995, funded by employer and employee contributions, mainly to enable the process of transferring workers from one job to another—the main benefit was a payment of half-pay for up to seven months for workers laid off.

Apart from these measures, social security is very tightly controlled and is very much a last resort for people with no chance of earning their own living or being looked after by their family. Government expenditure on social security is around 2.5 per cent of GDP.

Taiwan

Taiwan has had a social insurance scheme for military and government employees as well as a Labour Insurance Law since the 1950s. Under this there is a compulsory contribution split between employers (70 per cent), employees (20 per cent), and government (10 per cent). The scheme covers sickness, injury, maternity, old age, and death. It does not cover periods of unemployment. The scheme covers 7.6 million workers, or 35 per cent of the population. There is no unemployment benefit and a very residual social assistance provision. Social security takes up about 2.5 per cent of GDP.

Hong Kong[20]

The Hong Kong governments during the time of British rule prided themselves on a policy of 'positive non-intervention'.[21] The British government required that there should be no cost to the British treasury of any policies operated in the territory while local business interests ensured that there was a low level of personal and business taxation. Hence, except for a brief period in the early 1980s the government had a balanced budget or a surplus. This parsimony did not prevent an active government programme in public housing, education, and healthcare. The house-building programme, started in the 1950s, was accelerated in the early 1970s. By the end of the 1990s about 40 per cent of the population were living in government-owned flats and a further 20 per cent in owner-occupied flats which had been financed by the government. Over 90 per cent of healthcare was provided, mostly free of charge, by the Hospitals Authority. There is nine years of compulsory education, largely funded by government, and 18 per cent of school-leavers attend university in government-funded institutions.

However, as far as the alleviation of poverty and unemployment are concerned, the government is parsimonious. There is no unemployment benefit and no state-run pension scheme[22] and a rudimentary 'Comprehensive Social Security Assistance' scheme which provides a bare subsistence for otherwise destitute people.

POLITICS AND CULTURE: EXPLANATIONS OF 'ASIAN' WAYS OF WELFARE

The nature of the contractual relationship between an employer and an employee contains a great deal of variety. At one level, the employees of a firm in an export-processing zone in the Philippines, Thailand, or China may have a very pure form of exploitative relationship with the company. They live in minimally adequate conditions, work long hours, and have no reward outside their wages, either in health insurance, pensions, or whatever. At another level there are the permanent employees of a Japanese company or a Chinese state-owned enterprise, whose employment contract may include many rewards beyond the wages. Both relationships are contractual, but the latter set may go beyond what is strictly necessary to the interests of the employers. Accepting an obligation to an employee may generate a degree of loyalty, hard work, and self-sacrifice which would not come from wage-only employees. With increasing competition and the lowering of trade protection barriers, such obligations may become an unsustainable cost to the employers.

Have such obligations roots in some philosophical or 'cultural' tradition which is different from capitalism or at least from individual profit-maximizing behaviours? Has there ever been a similar contractual relationship between individuals and the state, in the sense that the state accepts certain contractual obligations in exchange for the duties that come with citizenship? In the region, such acceptance of obligations by governments has been quite rare. Where governments have been persuaded to accept some responsibility for the welfare of the citizens it has either been by encouraging them to work or having an obligation imposed by demands from temporarily powerful groups. These have included workers in times of labour shortages in the case of Korea, the urban labour élite in China, or in the case of Japan obligations demanded by the victorious in the War. The Japanese case of universal rights as opposed to rights based on position is an example of Western rather than Confucian principles being imposed from outside.

So, as far as special relationships are concerned, the only ones remaining are familial responsibility: neither the employment relationship nor the citizenship relationship seems to contain obligations beyond a contractual relationship, or at least when there is economic pressure on the relationship. In any case it has always applied only to an 'insider group' and not to an entire population.

This certainly seems to rule out the explanation of 'cultural' obligations from rulers to citizens. Obligations established through some innate notion of virtue are more common than rights established by law. Obligations are the mirror of rights: if someone is granted a right someone else has to accept the obligation and vice versa. Both can be established by law or by virtue. Welfare rights established by law and the obligations implied taken on by the state are an extreme case of people being asked (by paying tax) to take care of the welfare of strangers. Family obligations/rights established by virtue are not concerned with strangers—the only question is how far the obligation extends within the family and how far the family extends. In some rural societies there are different conventions, which cover extended and intermarried families and a scale of obligations.

A 'cultural' analysis would emphasize the variety of underlying attitudes to the family: intergenerational responsibilities in 'Confucian' societies, including Chinese, Japanese, and Korean people, are such that these people are self-reliant. Unfortunately, Japan, Korea, Taiwan, and China have the most developed levels of state involvement, and Christian and Muslim countries, such as the Philippines, Malaysia, and Indonesia the least developed.

A second set of explanations is socio-economic and essentially functionalist. As industrialization brings economic growth and urbanization, the traditional extended family is no longer able (and perhaps willing) to make intergenerational arrangements for old age and periods of unemployment. Migration to the cities breaks family ties while lower birth rates mean that there are fewer children to look after parents, while more 'instrumental' attitudes mean that people are more keen on their individual welfare than that of their parents and grandparents. Hence there is a gap in provision and the state automatically steps in to fill it. This is essentially an argument based on what happened in Western Europe after the depression of the 1930s and the Second World War. It is related to the idea that economic development generates political development and that a new class of middle-class people and professionals will demand more security organized by the state.

A third explanation is that those states which have made provision for pensions and unemployment insurance have made a compromise with organized labour. Certainly the development of state insurance schemes in Korea and Taiwan came after periods in which the trade unions became stronger and were making demands for the security of their members, either through employment rights or through welfare rights if companies were not made to guarantee employment. The authoritarian regime in Singapore is different: labour organization has not been strong, at least in recent decades, and there is high state involvement, especially in housing and through compulsory savings.

If the level of labour organization is an explanation for differences, it must take account of what organized labour has demanded: there are certain regimes in the region, which generate no trust. It would have been a foolhardy trade union leader who would ask a government such as that of Marcos, for example, to take care of saving for their members' old age. In these circumstances, if workers wanted to make collective provision, outside the family, they are unlikely to use state mechanisms for this collectivity: voluntary organization is more likely.

One of the arguments used by the people who proclaim globalization is that increased international competition makes it difficult for any one country to maintain a level of taxation which is very much out of line with its competitor nations. So, if a government wanted to have a public spending regime which has, say, a very large army or very high tax-funded pensions, this would mean that its companies would have to pay more tax than those in the competitor nations and the companies would either move or lose in competition. This implies that social provision (as well as the size of spending on other things) would converge, but at a low, competitive level. Politicians and owners of businesses in high-tax countries argue for tax reductions on the grounds of competitiveness.

The other argument about public spending relates specifically to welfare spending. In Japan there is a great fear of the European disease, which has many symptoms. The disincentive effects of unemployment benefits and the possible impact on savings of a state-funded pension scheme are seen as major reasons for lack of European competitiveness but also of the decline in morality and family values. While this position has been made public and official in Japan, it is a widely held view in the region that European decadence is closely linked to the effects of the 'welfare state' in its various European forms.

On the other hand, the last decade has seen a greater involvement of the state in matters previously considered a matter for the family, the individual, or the corporation. Aspects of social welfare, especially pensions and social security (but less so unemployment insurance) have become increasingly matters for states, whether at national or local level, in Japan, Korea, Taiwan, and Hong Kong. Singapore, in any case, has for many years had a rather special arrangement, the Provident Fund, mandated by the government, to take care of pensions and some housing and education financing.

So, is there a pattern? There are two possible general trends—one says that globalization and international competition forces state provision of 'welfare' downwards. Such a trend would be backed by explanations about the nature of the societies in which reliance on individuals and families is more common than reliance on the state. An alternative would be that economic growth and industrialization might produce welfare systems similar to those in the first wave of industrialization or similar to that in the USA. A third option would be that there is no general pattern in the region and the provision of social security, pensions, and healthcare may depend on specific local historical circumstances. So far, the third proposition seems to be most correct although the crisis revealed the vulnerability of societies that are used to employment growth when there is a sudden downturn in economic activity. As we have seen there was great variation in the degree to which social security and welfare systems were able to cope.

THE CRISIS: VULNERABILITY OF THE SELF-RELIANT SOCIETY IN MARKET DOWNTURNS

As the quotation from Dipak Dasgupta in Chapter 1 said, little attention was paid to the plight of the workers as the crisis hit, especially in Indonesia and Thailand. Social security schemes for periods of unemployment are in place in the richer countries in the region where there are also high savings rates. Low-paid workers who have migrated to work are in a poor position to survive economic downturns. There are three sources of the unemployment: the structural adjustments that happen when one industry falls on unprofitable times as has happened in microelectronics; the recessions resulting from overproduction or low demand; and the shift of certain industries from one location to another. If governments are unwilling or unable to do anything about these fluctuations in the demand for labour, they have to do something about the consequences. No government in the region wants to make provision for the welfare of long-term unemployed people. In the PRC the social security insurance system and institutions are a combination of payment with training and job placement. In the other countries that have unemployment insurance schemes they are time-limited. Where there are no unemployment insurance schemes, governments have to cope with the fact that there are likely to be periodic big increases in the numbers of unemployed people. In the case of the recent crisis nowhere were there adequate measures to keep the unemployed occupied or re-employed and the main policy response was one of maintenance of order.

NOTES

1. See e.g. R. Goodman, G. White, and H. J. Kwon, 'East Asian Social Policy: A Model to Emulate?' in *Social Policy Review*, 9 (Social Policy Association, UK). D. Jacobs, *Social Welfare Systems in East Asia: A Comparative Analysis Including Private Welfare* (London: Centre for Analysis of Social Exclusion, London School of Economics, 1998) examines private welfare provision.
2. See Chen Sheying, *Social Policy of the Economic State and Community Care in Chinese Culture: Ageing, Family, Urban Change and the Socialist Welfare Pluralism* (Aldershot, Brookfield: Avebury, 1996): 83.
3. See Chen Ai Ju and Gavin Jones, *Ageing in ASEAN: Its Socio-economic Consequences* (Singapore: Institute of Southeast Asian Studies, 1989).
4. Survey published by the Population Research Institute in 1988, reported in Chen Sheying, *Social Policy of the Economic State*: 286.
5. See I. Peng, *The Japanese Welfare State: Perspectives and Patterns of Change*, conference paper (Taiwan, 1998).
6. Ibid.
7. M. Takahashi, *The Emergence of Welfare Society in Japan* (Aldershot: Avebury, 1997) argues that one reason for more women working while they are married is that the cost of education has increased, making a second earner essential for educational progress in a private school.
8. Ibid. 226.
9. Kwon Huck-ju, *Inadequacy or Operational Failure? An Analysis of the Potential Crisis of the Korean National Pension Programme*, conference paper (Taiwan, 1998).
10. Milton Ezrati, *Asian Wall Street Journal*, 18 Nov. 1996.
11. The development of the various welfare regimes in Europe took individual courses, depending on local politics. Most ended with some notion of a settlement between workers, employers, and the state.
12. Takahashi, *The Emergence of Welfare Society in Japan*.
13. Goh Keng Swee, *The Practice of Economic Growth* (Singapore: Federal Publications, 1977).
14. Takahashi, *The Emergence of Welfare Society in Japan*: 48.

15. Ibid. 230–1.

16. Initially the contribution was 1% but it was revised up to 3% in 1998.

17. Jon S. T. Quah, *Singapore's Model of Economic Development: Lessons for Other Countries?*, conference paper (City University of Hong Kong, 1998).

18 See L. Low and T. C. Aw, *Housing a Healthy, Educated and Wealthy Nation through the CPF* (Singapore: Times Academic Press, 1997).

19. Including a 'Livelihood Protection Act', an 'Industrial Accident Compensation Scheme', etc.

20. For an analysis of social policy in Hong Kong see P. Wilding, A. S. Huque, and L. P. J. Tao (eds.), *Social Policy in Hong Kong* (Cheltenham: Edward Elgar, 1997).

21. A phrase attributed to P. Haddon-Cave, Financial Secretary.

22. A Mandatory Provident Scheme was started in 1997 but will take a long time before there are any pensioner beneficiaries.

Managing the Network State

One aspect of the argument about convergence is that there is growing similarity in the way in which the state is managed through the spread of knowledge about how other people manage in other countries. This knowledge transfer could be made because bureaucrats in one country read about or visit their counterparts elsewhere or because of the actions and advice of multinational management consultants whose solutions are based on ideal types rather than national characteristics. A third influence is the international organizations, such as the World Bank or the IMF, making loans conditional on certain management and governance practices.

One homogenizing tendency has been to privatize state assets and functions through sales or contracting out. While there has been by no means a uniform set of privatization, there has certainly been a tendency towards divestment. There has also been, in most countries, a search for improved accountability and better performance management and measurement, both at individual and organizational levels. Such features may be defined as 'good governance' or a set of practices likely to produce efficiency and accountability and generate business confidence in a nation's civil service institutions.

Part of this tendency has been reinforcement of, or a move towards, merit as a principle for recruitment to and advancement within civil services. While some civil services have had competitive recruitment for a long time, such as Japan, Singapore, and Malaysia, others, such as China, have recruited and then preferred for promotion people with party connections. The Chinese government is moving slowly in the direction of competitive recruitment and promotion on merit.

Superficially it looks as if all governments are doing the same things since many use the same rhetoric, at least in their materials translated into English. There has been a long history of 'reforms' in many countries, some of which use the same techniques and the same managerial language as management changes in the public service in the USA, Europe, and Australasia. They are talking of increased efficiency, shedding functions through privatization, reducing bureaucracy, and improving accountability.

DIFFERENCES AMONG STATES

In practice, the 'reforms' have different agendas in different countries, depending on who is calling for the reforms, which factions and ministries are in favour or otherwise of the changes, the current management practices, the organizational culture which has been inherited, and the events which create the opportunity for change.

One underlying variation in the region is that the role of the public sector varies between countries. Whereas in Japan, Korea, and Singapore, the civil service has been in a leading role in partnership with business in making investment decisions, this has not been such a significant function in Hong Kong, Indonesia, or the Philippines. In China the civil service is very extensive and the organizations which run the state-owned enterprises, though called 'ministries', are more like an integrated management structure than a ministry and relatively autonomous state enterprises. Civil servants and party officials take all the main planning and investment decisions. This has been true in other places as well, to the extent that the networks among politicians and civil servants make the distinctions between state and business unclear.[1]

Another difference is in the scale of the public sector workforce. Table 7.1 shows the ratio of public sector employment to population and total employment in a selection of countries in the region.

Table 7.1 Population and public service numbers, 1994–1995

	Public servants	Population (m.)	Workforce (m.)	PS as % of population	PS as % of workforce
PRC	40m	1.2bn	620	3.3	6.4
Indonesia	4m	187	81	2.1	4.9
Japan	3.25m	126	66	2.6	4.9
Philippines	1.2m	64.8	28	1.9	4.3
Malaysia	0.7m	22	8	3.2	8.7
Singapore	60k[a]	3	1.7	2	3.5
Hong Kong	190k	6.3	3.1	3	6.2
Taiwan	584k	21	9.2	3.6	6.3

[a]Civil service only
Sources: various

As well as differences in scale, there are other underlying differences between the public sectors in the region. They are partly a result of the history of the development of the civil services during periods of foreign occupation, whether by European colonial powers, by the USA (in the case of the Philippines), by the Japanese, or by the Allied forces in Japan. In the region, only Thailand has not been subject to foreign occupation in modern times. This legacy gives certain features: recruitment, structures, rules. This is not to

argue that these systems are immutable, rather that history generates attitudes and behaviours among public servants. In many cases the legacy was
one of corruption, as colonial administrators used their power for personal
enhancement.

In some places the civil service or its institutions are used in the political
process of building constituencies and support. In Japan and China, and to
some extent Indonesia, ministries and commissions are both the means
through which politics are conducted and the prize. Factions capture and use
parts of the bureaucracy for their own ends. In other administrations, the ruling party or élite manages to control the whole bureaucratic apparatus. When
'reforms' involve structural changes, such as closing down ministries or merging them, as has been recently proposed in China and Japan, some powers of
factions are enhanced and others diminished.

As well as political factional politics, there are differences in the way in
which bureaucrats gain or lose power and which departments are dominant.
Ministries of Finance are traditionally the most powerful department in a civil
service and often initiate reform processes, sometimes to retain or enhance
their own power. In other places, personnel ministries or civil service commissions are more powerful and they will start a reform process. This shapes the
nature of the changes and influences the implementation process.

These political institutional constraints lead us to question the convergence
or homogenization thesis. For example, there may be an economic rationality
to decentralizing financial control and reducing the detailed powers of a
finance ministry; the logic will only be followed if the power of the finance
ministry can be eroded. This is as true in France as it is in Japan. Similarly, a
'modern' approach to personnel management might suggest devolving many
personnel matters to line management and reducing the power of central personnel departments. Whether this happens or not depends on whether the
personnel department is willing or is forced to give up its power. A 'historical
institutionalist' perspective would suggest that these rigidities caused by
power-holding are broken only occasionally and then by changes large
enough to cause a crisis.[2] What remains to be seen from the current economic
crisis is whether it results in sufficient change in power structures to make a
fundamental difference to power relations within public services and between
civil services and other power bases in society.

Features that may be identified as 'national' cultures, although some may
be common to more than one nation or nationality, also affect the organizational culture of civil services. Attitudes to hierarchy and seniority, to obedience, to uncertainty will not only influence how the organizations are
managed but will also act as a constraint on change. For example, if there is a
tradition of promotion by seniority and staff are happy with it, it is very difficult to introduce pay and promotion schemes based on merit or performance.
The Japanese civil service, for example, has found it difficult to promote
people above their seniors. The Hong Kong civil service has a performance
appraisal scheme, which would only work if people could break the cultural

norm of maintaining harmony at work by not confronting problems or conflicts.

A sixth source of differences is scale and geography. Unitary government is
less likely in big states, especially when there are geographic power bases.
Chinese provinces, Malaysian states, Korean regions, and Japanese regions
have administrative units reflecting these interests. Relatively autonomous
tiers of government are likely to resist central-government-sponsored reform
programmes and are likely to have their own change agendas.

While this list of sources of difference does not exhaust the explanations for
variation among civil services, it does suggest that there are powerful forces
against homogenization. If all six apply, there would be strong reasons for
doubting whether some universal model could ever be applied in the place
where this is the case.

TRENDS BEFORE THE CRISIS

The public sector and economic development

The model of the 'developmental state' was developed in Japan and Korea. It
seems that there were special circumstances in both places which led to the
close links between government and business and the banks, which was not
transferable to other countries. Recent events in both places show that in the
very long run, the closeness between politicians, civil servants, and banks led
to corruption, or was definable as corrupt from the beginning.

However, the idea of the civil service as an engine for economic development was an important influence on other governments. In Malaysia, the
'look east' policy which tried to create 'Malaysia Incorporated' was clearly
based on an interpretation of Japan's way of managing the relationship
between business and government. Civil servants were urged to think in the
national interest and be cooperative with business.[3] The director-general of
the public services department claimed 'the Civil Service of Malaysia has
grown from being "Law and Order"-oriented in the 1960s into one that is a
pacesetter and facilitator for national development in the 1990s.'[4]

Thailand initiated reforms in 1991 with a similar aim—to make the civil service more cooperative with business. The Indonesian civil service, with political connections, has been active in promoting economic growth and
sponsoring development

Controlling the size of the civil service

Even before the crisis-induced measures of 1998, several governments had a
concern that their civil services had grown excessively and without control.

Japan had managed to control the growth of its central-government bureaucracy[5] (although not local-government employee numbers) by simply passing a law limiting the number of employees. The Thai government passed a law in 1980 limiting the growth of civil service personnel to 2 per cent per annum but this did not stop the growth of 30 per cent over the next decade.[6]

In Indonesia there was an even greater growth in the number of civil servants, from 1.6 million in 1974 to 2.7 million in 1984 and over 4 million in 1994, at which point a zero-growth policy was adopted.[7]

Hong Kong has had a policy of keeping growth in public expenditure to the rate of growth of GDP but has also had an implied policy of keeping civil service numbers under control.

Japan had also announced its planned reductions in the size of the civil service before the economic crisis. Different political parties made various 'bids' of percentage reductions in the scale of the civil service. While not attributable to the financial crisis of 1997, the slowdown in the Japanese economy and the diminishing confidence in the civil service had led to these calls for cuts in civil service numbers.

Singapore removed 'headcount control' in 1997 and replaced it with financial control. Departments can hire as many people as they want while staying within their cash limit. Singapore was the only state in the region to have abandoned concern with the numbers employed and adopted financial control instead. This difference can be accounted for by the fact that Singapore has a financial control system that is accurate and effective and that there has been no political issue about the size of the civil service as there has been in other places.

Changes in personnel management practices

Governments are trying to improve the quality of staff by open, competitive recruitment (standard practice in Japan, Singapore, and HK, and innovative in the PRC). The PRC claims that this is working well and receives ten qualified applicants for each position, a similar ratio to Japan's. There is also a decrease in automatic promotion through seniority. Only Malaysia now has widespread use of seniority for promotion but there have been official announcements that this is going to change.

In Japan there has also been an attempt to introduce promotion on merit but among the top civil servants there is still a strong expectation that people do not get promoted above their seniors.

Singapore government increased the pay of its civil servants and indexed it to salaries in specific occupations in the private sector, from 1989. At the same time the proportion of the benefits package in pension and medical benefits was reduced and the pensions were converted into a contribution to the CPF. This was thought to improve flexibility, allowing people to move jobs without loss of pension rights. There is also a bonus scheme, based on performance appraisal. Ninety-five per cent of staff get graded a to c on a five-point scale, in which c is enough for the standard bonus. Maximum bonus is 50 per cent of annual salary; 10 per cent are graded a and 25 per cent b, which is defined as 'far exceeds the requirements of the substantive grade'.[8]

In Japan salaries are currently decided by the personnel department, using private sector comparisons. Work effort, indicators of performance, are not taken into account, nor is there an appraisal scheme.

Singapore and Japan represent two approaches to the problem of pay in a system where it is culturally difficult for one civil servant to judge another. In Singapore, almost everyone gets the standard bonus, in Japan there is no appraisal. What is interesting is that in both cases, senior managers are concerned about the link between pay and performance but cannot implement a scheme.

Hong Kong falls between the two: there is an appraisal scheme which is used to determine promotion (but not bonuses), but managers and staff believe that the performance bandings are not well related to measurable performance.

The PRC has a bonus scheme, based on annual appraisal. The bonuses are awarded for the achievement of targets but the appraisal system is a participatory one, in which peers are involved in the process.

Reducing corruption and decronyfication[9]

Japan, China, Malaysia, and Korea have all recently demonstrated some of the bad effects of a too close connection between business and government: loans, which caused bankruptcy, strategic industries which have been inefficient, etc. The attempt to make a 'clean' administration can affect recruitment, external scrutiny, and openness in decision-making.

Hong Kong had an anti-corruption campaign in the 1970s and established the Independent Commission against Corruption. Anti-corruption measures are now a matter of routine rather than special campaigns

China has had a series of anti-corruption campaigns, leading to many arrests and executions. At the Party Congress in September 1997 the Discipline Inspection Commission of the Chinese Communist Party Central Committee reported that its investigations had resulted in 120,000 cadres being expelled from the party and that in the five years from October 1992 to June 1997 a total of 7.55 million complaints had been lodged against allegedly corrupt officials. Some of the prosecutions, such as that of the Mayor of Beijing, were very public events.

One of the reasons for Singapore's increase in salaries in 1989 was to try to make sure that public servants were paid enough to keep them from the temptation to take bribes.

'Customer orientation'

Many countries have had campaigns to improve the quality of service at the interface with the customer. Singapore has had its work improvement teams which are like quality circles. There is a PS21[10] campaign with a loose instruction to ministries to find their own way of making service improvements. The government reported that it had received over 500,000 ideas about quality improvement during 1997.

Japan started a 'Polite and Considerate Public Services Campaign' in 1988 and established the Polite and Considerate Public Services Promotion Council.

Malaysia's public services have all been instructed to apply for ISO 9000 registration in an attempt to improve service quality. However, probably to make registration easier, there is a special version for Malaysia, called MS 9000.

Hong Kong civil service has published performance pledges for each department, setting out quality standards (mostly waiting times) for all its services. In almost all cases, these targets are achieved at 95 per cent plus and the targets are not adjusted upwards, except when they are significantly over-achieved.

Singapore has a system of performance targets. The incentive to meet the targets is the right to carry over 5 per cent of budgets if 85 per cent of the targets are met.

Political control and the civil service

Prime Minister Hashimoto's changes to the civil service in Japan were an attempt to re-establish political control over the bureaucracy. It has been said that in Japan 'the politicians reign while the bureaucrats rule'.[11] By changing the functions of ministries and abolishing and merging them he thought that seats of power would be destroyed and politicians would have more control over what the government did. It could be that the new, larger ministries are even bigger seats of factional and bureaucrat power.

One of the reasons for the reform of the Chinese civil service was the opposite: to enhance the independence of bureaucrats from politicians. The idea was accepted by the People's Congress in 1987 that people should be appointed for their competence rather than their connections and that they should be left to get on with their jobs without interference. In the implementation of this policy that objective was reversed. Lam and Chan argued[12] that Li Peng thought that the bureaucracy had too much independence and stability and should be subject to more political control, much like Hashimoto.

In Malaysia, UMNO politicians for a long time consisted of ex-civil servants and there was therefore a very close relationship between party and bureaucracy.

REFORMING STATE MANAGEMENT IN CHINA AND JAPAN

The civil service has been central to the development of China and Japan. In China, hierarchies ran from individual factories through their sponsoring ministries to the top of government. While the Japanese civil service was never in direct control of industries, it played an important part during the developmental state period. In both countries there have been changes in the way in which the civil service is managed. The two examples show some of the difficulties involved in moving civil service organizations towards a mode of rule that is rational and technocratic and away from one that is based, in part at least, on personal connections and favours.

People's Republic of China

During the Mao era there were three kinds of bureaucrat: administrators, technocrats, and 'politicrats'. They worked in government agencies, public organizations, and industrial enterprises.[13] In the early revolutionary period, people were recruited according to their family background and 'revolutionary experience' rather then their qualifications and competence to do their job. The Cultural Revolution removed intellectuals and replaced them with people with revolutionary zeal. Thus, the economic transformation after 1978 posed two problems for the leadership: the cadres in charge of agencies and enterprises had been chosen for their commitment to the previous, Maoist ideas about how the economy should be run and they had not been selected because of their competence. A prerequisite for implementing the economic reforms was therefore to replace these cadres and in the decade to 1992 over 6 million veterans were replaced.

David Lampton[14] set out some of the problems of implementing policy changes faced by the Deng government. These included the fact that the policy-making process relied on the laborious development of consensus which meant change was slow; the problem of the 'independent kingdoms' which resisted any threat to their status and in turn to the factions which controlled them;[15] and the fact that many agencies were involved in any policy change. Within these constraints, the Deng administration included management and administrative changes as part of its policy of transforming China, thinking that changes in civil service attitudes and practices would be necessary to implement the economic reforms.

There have been four[16] aspects of public sector changes in the PRC: making state-owned enterprises more subject to market pressures and less direct control from their parent ministry or organ; separation of the party from the government; horizontal and vertical devolution of responsibilities; and administrative reforms. The administrative reforms included reorganizing the structure of government and the establishment of what was called a 'civil service system'. This last had the objectives, which are familiar themes of 'new public management', of separating management from politics, improving performance through recruitment based on ability, and changes to the pay system. There was also a desire to reduce the number of people employed in various aspects of the bureaucracy by 25 per cent.

The idea of creating an independent civil service, whose members would have stability of employment, rather than being attached to political factions was accepted by the People's Congress in 1987. The idea was to create a separate class of non-political civil servants (who would work in parallel with political ones) who would be recruited by competitive examination, rather than through the cadre system. They would be permanent and thus offer some policy stability amid political instability. The policy had some successes. Zhou's[17] study showed that political background became less significant than competence, especially for 'technocrats', if not for 'politicrats'.

The political process of implementation changed these objectives. First, the examinations were established but recruitment to senior and middle positions was considered to be a transfer and therefore open only to existing cadres.[18] In any case, recruitment was not entirely open, as only those eligible to live[19] in Beijing could take the exams to work in Beijing and similarly for other posts at provincial level.[20]

There were also pay changes, which were intended to maintain some comparability for civil servants with salaries in the emerging sectors, to create a distinctive civil service, and to relate pay to performance. In practice, the pay changes were extended to all cadres, removing the distinctiveness.

What happened in the process of implementation, which spanned the Tiananmen events, was that stability as an objective was abandoned: 'Li Peng and the post-Tiananmen Square leadership evidently had a sharply different understanding of the main problems of China's state bureaucracy. While Zhao Ziyang and his aides traced the root of the problem to the lack of stability and policy continuity and the unnecessarily high degree of political influence, Li Peng faulted the bureaucracy for possessing too much stability.'[21] Lam and Chan (1996) conclude that the changes as implemented produced a very limited departure from the old cadre management system and that the attempt to separate administration from politics was given much less emphasis.

This is not to say that there have not been changes. Interviews in Beijing[22] showed that people in the Ministry of Personnel at least believed that the entrance examinations were having an impact and that performance was being improved by changes to the personnel system, especially the appraisal process. For example, one interviewee told me that the system of dismissal for cadres who perform badly was taking effect, and 2,000 had been dismissed in 1995. The open recruitment system was also working, with 760 jobs openly advertised. It is clear that the radical move of creating a relatively autonomous civil service, staffed purely on merit and rewarded on performance, has been only partially implemented. More recently, the government has claimed that the examination system has opened up the civil service to recruitment on merit. The Xinhua news agency reported in January 1998 that since the 1993 regulations on civil servants were issued nine exams had been held and 3,000 civil servants had been recruited to central government posts from 40,000 candidates. At lower levels of administration 53,000 positions had been filled by competitive examination by 530,000 candidates. The same report claimed that 664 of the recruits were people who changed their residential status to take up their new jobs and that 2,636 were peasants.

There is a tension between the leadership's desire for control over policy and its need for efficient implementation. Different parts of the leadership are attached to particular parts of the state apparatus and like to staff their parts with their people. As elsewhere, an independent, unattached civil service may be an ideal and an officially stated objective but the realities of politics compromise the ideal, especially when decisions are made about whom should be hired and promoted within the policy-making parts of the bureaucracy.

Japan

Superficially, Japan has been 'reforming' its public sector since the First Provisional Commission for Administrative Reform was established in 1962, which was concerned with the size of the public sector and its productivity improvement, compared with the private sector.[23] From that time on there has been a concern to contain the numbers employed and the amount of spending on the public sector. While we should not be misled by figures on public spending, which generally exclude spending by local authorities (and the recent fiscal crisis in Japan is evidence of problems), the scale of central government employment has stayed fairly constant since the numbers were 'capped' in 1967. Containment was partly achieved by transferring responsibility to sectors not included in the central government accounts.

A second Provisional Commission was set up in 1981, still concerned with scale and spending, themes which have persisted through subsequent 'reform' efforts. The other themes which the government has pursued have been some denationalization ('reform' of the railways was started in 1984 and they were privatized in 1987, after staff had been reduced and long-term debt disposed of), an attempt at decentralization since 1993, as well as certain moves towards deregulation and the promotion of efficiency.

There is also pressure to reduce bribery and corruption in Japan. The public cases of bribe-taking which emerged during the 1997/8 crisis were a real political embarrassment. The arrest of two Ministry of Finance bank inspectors in January 1998 and the subsequent resignation of the minister and vice-minister brought renewed calls for tighter laws on corruption which were resisted by the prime minister who said: 'It is regrettable that it became clear that moral codes were not enough to penetrate the conduct of civil servants. I hope civil servants will reflect upon their actions and renew their mission to serve the public.' [24] After these events, a start was made on drawing up a law to formulate an ethical code for public servants.

These actions to reduce corruption are partly symbolic and partly an attempt to break the strong connections between public servants and business. If they are followed through, they will represent a 'modernization' in the sense that decisions should be made on rational, economic grounds rather than because of the connections between officials and businesses.

In Japan in recent years, there have officially been efforts to improve public management in response to political and public concern about the civil service. Kaneko[25] reported the five main areas of change to the International Institute of Administrative Sciences Round Table in 1997. The first was concerned with simplicity and 'responsiveness to the new age'. One aspect of this was the familiar cry for a smaller civil service. After the fiscal problems of 1996/7 and the spate of scandals about public officials at central and local level during 1996, there was competition among the political parties to trim the public sector, whether the number of agencies and departments or the number of employees. The Democratic Party of Japan put in the highest (lowest) bid of a 50 per cent cut in employment. An official target was adopted, a reduction of 35,000 of the 855,000 between 1997 and 2001. This may seem surprising, since Japan had for nearly three decades managed to keep the size of the central civil service small, under the 1969 Law Concerning the Fixed Numbers of Personnel of Administrative Organs. The idea of further reducing the numbers employed was not new—this was the ninth plan to do so.

The second change was another attempt to improve the accountability and management of Public Corporations. Half a million people were employed in the ninety or so national public corporations (in 1994) and there were 6,600 local public corporations.[26]

The third proposal under this rubric was the interchange of civil servants among departments 'to decrease the ill-effects of departmentalism in the central government'.[27] As well as the problem of civil servants becoming narrowly focused, this proposal also has political implications: ministries and Bureaux as seats of factional political power rely on 'their' civil servants to compete for resources and attention. Moving civil servants would diminish their loyalties and make them less useful competitors.

The second main area of change was another familiar item to observers of administrative 'reforms':[28] the idea that public servants should be allowed and encouraged to take more initiative and accept more responsibility. In Japan's case this was to include reducing the amount of regulation and devolving more authority to subnational levels of government.

The third set of changes were about openness and trust, in response to the scandals and secrecy which had been part of the bad publicity for the public sector. Here the main ideas were to give the public more access to information, a tightening of the implementation of Administrative Procedures Law to ensure due process, and a commitment to improve discipline and increase the amount of inspection to avoid scandals. The role of inspections in other areas was also to be increased. There were also proposals to improve service quality through better use of technology and a Polite and Considerate Public Services Campaign.

The Administrative Reform Council made proposals to reorganize and privatize. The areas which the Council proposed for possible privatization included mail delivery, postal savings and life insurance services, ports and harbours, parts of the hospital service, universities, and so on. The Management and Co-ordination Agency developed a formula for deciding which activities of government should be public and which should be in the private sector. This 'neutral' analysis generally says that if functions can be privatized or contracted out they should be, but policy work and advice should stay within the public sector. There were also proposals to make some organizations, such as the mint, into independent bodies.[29] In September 1997 Hashimoto appointed a new head of the Management and Coordination Agency. He needed somebody who could command the support of enough politicians and departmental and agency heads to implement the proposed changes. He chose Koko Sato who had such support, although his appointment was treated with derision by the opposition.[30] The government faced a variety of problems in implementing both management changes and privatization. Hashimoto had made much of the need for administrative reform in the election campaign and was expected to be keen on implementation. He was not the first prime minister to do so. Prime Minister Suzuki (1980–2) had said 'I will stake my political life on administrative reform.'[31]

The political pressures for change are strong. The support which the civil service received during the thirty years of rapid economic growth is no longer as strong. While the civil service probably accepted too much praise for the strength of the growth, they are now probably receiving an unfair share of the blame for the slowdown. The fiscal crisis has not been caused by an inefficient civil service, but by spending on infrastructure projects and agricultural subsidies which have been necessary to build coalitions strong enough to stay in power without raising the taxes to finance these expenditures, which would have threatened popular support. It was pointed out to me that even if the whole of the central civil service were scrapped tomorrow, it would save less than 1 per cent on sales tax.

While increases in efficiency would not solve the fiscal problem, there is a feeling that civil servants are too protected. Most have a job for life, a luxury available to a decreasing number of Japanese as companies change their employment practices. Many senior civil servants, especially from the Ministry of Finance, have been given post-retirement positions in public corporations or companies with whom they established relationships while working. One of the most recent proposals has been to 'establish an administration that is open and trusted by the people' (Kaneko). The proposals here are simply that people should act according to the rules, not accept bribes, and be subjected to inspections. To have to call such actions 'reform' is a sign that the civil service is not trusted. There is no 'reform' which states that politicians should follow the same code.

There are three main obstacles to real change in the Japanese civil service. The first is political. In Japan the post-office postal savings bank is one of the biggest deposit holders in the world and can provide loans which are very valuable sources of influence for those who control it. To take such an institution out of the control of a political faction would require a very powerful prime minister. This applies also to structural changes, such as the reduction in the number of ministries and bureaux, each of which is a source of power for a faction. While a majority of the ruling Liberal Democratic Party may favour change, reform should only apply to those parts controlled by another faction. A civil servant told me 'the accumulation of exceptions is a barrier to reform.'

The main barrier to fundamental managerial change is the entrenched system of recruitment, promotion, and pay. While good quality recruits are forthcoming through the system of competitive examinations, and the civil service is an increasingly popular career choice as prospects in private companies become less certain, promotion is largely on seniority and pay is determined by incremental scales. A 'job for life' is still possible in the Japanese civil service. This is felt by some to put a constraint on improving performance through better management.

The third is the degree of autonomy of local government. As well as ministries and bureaux, factions gain strength from local authorities. While the employment of central civil servants is controlled by the 1969 Law Concerning the Fixed Numbers of Personnel Administrative Organs and has been kept down to around 850,000, local authority employment rose from 2.2 million in the mid-1960s to 3.3 million in 1997. While central government technically had the powers to control local authorities, especially when they were implementing policy through delegated powers, in practice mayors and governors have been relatively autonomous.

Lessons from China and Japan

In both China and Japan the change programmes were rooted in some similar causes: the Chinese government said that civil services needed to change in order to make possible the economic reforms, while the Japanese government similarly thought that economic slowdown made civil service reform necessary; both wanted to reduce the size of the civil service for reasons of expense and to change the power relations between civil servants and politicians. Similarly, some of the approaches to performance improvement were similar: trying to relate reward and enhancement to performance; shifting the balance of activities between the state and the private sector; and trying to improve the performance and accountability of public enterprises and public corporations.

In a sense, they both suffered from the same implementation problems. In both cases it was difficult to separate the management of the state and its organizations from the processes of competition for power between factions. The main difference, superficially, was that the administrative changes in Japan were made the subject of election campaigns, a process which did not occur so publicly in China, but there is no doubt that the Chinese changes were political, in the sense that different factions had different ideas about the relative autonomy of the civil service from parties and factions. Some factions might be able to consolidate their power through the changes. These debates also occurred in Japan.

These examples show that there are still culturally specific management practices and that reforms are often superficial or ritualistic while old behaviours and relationships persist. In other words, if the network relationships are fundamentally hierarchical and strong, then these power relationships will survive formal or official attempts at changes in practice. If networks are based on familial or other expressive ties, and these ties are stronger than the official, hierarchical relationships, then attempts to impose official, instrumental ties over the familial or expressive ones will fail. The forces benefiting from such arrangements will resist the attempt both to replace one network with another and to replace the network with more instrumental connections of market or hierarchy demanding performance.

Suganuma[32] has pointed out the similarities between the structures of the state in Japan and the PRC. Despite the political differences between the two states, there are many institutional similarities. Both have a hierarchical structure of relationships which operates both through official positions and through personal hierarchy, mainly based on seniority. Both systems use personal connections to achieve results and personal advancement and both use patron–client relationships to form and maintain competing factions. Patronage enables senior people to build their own networks of connections, which may endure even after official reorganizations are carried out. The organizational form in both cases is that of networks of connections operating within an official hierarchy. The connections may not be formally recognized but everyone working in the organizations knows that they exist alongside the formal hierarchy. The connections cross the boundary between those who are elected and those who are appointed, in the case of Japan and between the party and the organs of the state in the case of China.

What these two examples show is that management arrangements within the state apparatus embody the way in which connections are made and maintained. In the economic field a shift from governance by expressive ties and connections to governance by market relationships involves a fundamental change in social relations. Similarly, a change from rule by connections, networks, and patronage to rule by hierarchy and impartiality involves a change in the social relations within the civil service and within its networks connecting the state and other parts of society.

THE CRISIS AND PUBLIC MANAGEMENT

As we saw in Chapter 1 the economic difficulties in the region did not all start in 1997. The Chinese government had faced an impending crisis of the falling profitability and mounting social liabilities of their state-owned enterprises since around 1990. Similarly the Japanese government and especially its civil service had faced a crisis of slower growth since 1989. It would be too simple to say that the 1997 economic difficulties induced sudden, radical changes in the way in which all the civil services in the region were managed.

The economic and financial problems in Asia since mid-1997 produced some budget and staff cuts and calls for improved efficiency from the public services of the region. Revelations of corrupt practices and close ties between officials and business in some of the countries have also caused calls from some for greater accountability and more openness. While these calls may not be new the crisis challenged the power of previously impervious civil servants and may have created the conditions for real changes. They certainly dispelled some of the illusions about dispassionate technocrats in Japan, working for the good of national development and ignoring personal gain. No one had illusions about the separation of government and business in Indonesia but the crisis threw into relief the extent of the connections.

China's recent announcements about the changes to the structure of ministries is a move in the opposite direction to those in Malaysia. The Chinese government says that it wants the civil service to take care of macroeconomic management and the regulatory framework rather than get involved in the details of businesses and their investment decisions. It could be that the result of the financial crisis is that a similar thing happens in Japan and Korea although it is too early to tell.

The economic crisis especially in Indonesia, Thailand, and Korea, all of whose governments had to borrow from the IMF, resulted in accelerated privatization and reduction in public spending. The three governments which had to borrow from the IMF sent 'letters of intent'[33] setting out their programmes which they offered in exchange for the loans. Thailand's letter detailed a cut in public spending of 100 billion baht, or just under 2 per cent of GDP, and increases in tax on alcohol, tobacco, cars, and luxury goods in order to make a fiscal surplus of 1 per cent of GDP. Indonesia also made a plan in November 1997 to create a fiscal surplus of 1 per cent of GDP but abandoned the idea by January 1998 as infeasible. It also promised to reduce government's involvement in industry. Korea, in its policies announced for the standby arrangement in December 1997, announced that it would aim for a balanced budget or a small surplus for 1998.

The PRC made the most dramatic proposals to reduce the number of ministries and civil servants in March 1998. A plan was announced to the National People's Congress to scrap fifteen ministry-level bodies and create fewer, smaller ministries. The main diagnosis was that the ministries at the head of industries (such as coal, power, metallurgical industry, machine building, electronics, chemicals, etc.) were no longer useful if the enterprises they supervised were to operate commercially and make their own investment decisions. Announcing the changes, cabinet secretary Luo Gan also implied that one of the reasons that the state-owned enterprise sector was in such bad shape was that poor investment decisions had been made by the parent ministries.

The Chinese newspaper *Wen Hui Bao* also reported that the size and cost of the bureaucracy, whatever its efficiency or otherwise, was no longer supportable. The number of government staff had grown by 82 per cent since the economic reforms started in 1978, while the population had grown by 27 per cent.

In January 1998 Malaysia's government froze the appointment of new staff to the civil service and announced various cosmetic austerity measures, curbing overseas travel and entertainment expenses. In an unintended irony the government also announced that because of financial hard times it was abandoning the plan to set up a new department to implement bureaucratic reform.

Korea's new government announced in January 1998 that it was planning to cut 17,612 jobs out of a total of 161,855 over a period of three years as an austerity measure.

CONVERGENCE: THE END OF RULE BY CONNECTIONS?

There is no doubt that politicians and public officials talk to each other around the world and there is a high level of awareness of other countries' practices. Chinese officials visited France and Canada when they designed their 'civil service system'. Singapore officials went to new Zealand to look at accruals accounting and output-based budgeting: they decided against accruals but learned about output-based budgeting which became 'budgeting for results'. The Hong Kong government made extensive use of international consultants in its 'serving the community' campaign, which was also influenced by the UK charter initiative, through Governor Patten. Japanese officials visited the UK and elsewhere when designing their version of executive agencies.

Malaysia seems to have followed all the fashions it can find and uses the jargon. For example: '[the Chief Secretary] has strived [*sic*] to transform the Civil Service into a customer-focused, mission-driven, performance-based and proactive force that remains responsive and accountable'.[34] In addition 'Look east' and Vision 2020 were explicitly based on Mahatir's interpretation of the Japanese version of the developmental state.

The motivations for change in the different countries are not the same. When management changes are adopted locally, the form the changes take depends partly on fashion, partly on the problem the changes are designed to solve and partly on the underlying organizational culture.

Singapore and Hong Kong have never had a fiscal crisis. Neither borrows, even for capital projects, and normally both have a fiscal surplus. And yet both have had serious efforts at improving efficiency and effectiveness. By contrast, Japan has the biggest fiscal deficit in the OECD. A programme of reducing public sector running costs would do very little to address that problem which was caused by spending on infrastructure projects and agricultural subsidies which were not funded by tax rises for political reasons. Some of the calls for economy or financial stringency come from moral or ideological grounds rather than economic necessity.

In Japan (at local authority level), China, and Indonesia the numbers employed in the civil service seem to have grown (from the mid-1980s to the mid-1990s) without this being an explicit government policy. Part of the motivation of change programmes was to control and possibly reverse this tendency. There are institutional constraints on programmes of management change in the public sector. Japanese government attempts at privatizing the post-office savings bank (for example) was resisted by the vested factional interest which benefited from the bank (the biggest deposit-taker in Japan)

Early efforts to replace the cadre system of civil service recruitment in China with a competitive, merit-based system were stopped or delayed by the cadres inventing obstacles and ways around the system, such as reclassifying promotions as transfers.

In Malaysia, despite the jargon and the campaigns on public service, there is still corruption and nepotism that get in the way of serious reforms. Powerful ministries can resist changes which threaten their power. Despite formal devolution of recruitment and bonus payments in Singapore, for example, the personnel department still has a great deal of central power. There are cultural impediments to changes to systems that require reward or promotion according to performance rather than seniority. These various impediments to change might be described as 'cultural' constraints to changes in the way civil services are managed. In all cases they are examples of the strength of existing connections' resistance to the introduction of more 'rational' ways of working.

If there really were homogenization of management practices, whether caused by globalization or by the diffusion of practice, then we would expect to find evidence of it in those countries which are most exposed to international influence or pressure. Management ideas flow freely and there are governments powerful enough to implement changes in the machinery of government and management structures and processes. In other words, the conditions for convergence are in place.

In a discussion of the credibility of convergence of management, Lawrence Lynn[35] argues that there is more convergence of the 'meta-language' with which the changes are described than in the changes themselves. He also argues that the changes are mostly modest, that they result from national political considerations rather then international influence and that the biggest change is in the privatization of state-owned enterprises.

So far evidence suggests that there are only a few elements of convergence, centred on trying to improve performance and trying to keep costs and numbers employed under control. Each government is trying to find its own solutions, within its own constraints of politics, relationships, resistance to change, and organizational and national culture. If there is a general reform tendency, it is away from rule by connections and towards a combination of rule by power or hierarchy and rule by market. When politicians have tried to curb the power of civil servants they have been trying to use their formal power to overturn the power of the connected networks of civil servants and their sponsors. Most of the reforms of personnel matters, such as recruitment and promotion by competitive examination and performance pay, are examples of trying to introduce a more market-oriented approach. The tensions and problems of implementation are mainly caused by the resistance of the established networks to the ending of rule by connections.

NOTES

1. See M. Orrù, N. W. Biggart, and G. G. Hamilton, *The Economic Organization of East Asian Capitalism.*
2. See K. Thelen and S. Steinmo, 'Historical Institutionalism in Comparative Politics', in S. Steinmo, K. Thelen, and F. Longstreth (eds.), *Structuring Politics: Historical Institutionalism in Comparative Analysis* (Cambridge: Cambridge University Press, 1992).
3. Some of the 'Malaysia Incorporated' changes were fairly basic, e.g. development Administration circular no. 2, 1991, urged civil servants to make meetings work better and to produce minutes. A. Sarji, *The Changing Civil Service: Malaysia's Competitive Edge* (Selangor: Darul Ehsan, Pelanduk Publications, 1993): 6.
4. Dato' Dr Mazlan bin Ahmad, in the preface to A. Sarji, *Civil Service Reforms: Towards Malaysia's Vision 2020* (Selangor: Darul Ehsan, Pelanduk Publications, 1996).
5. Through the 'Law Concerning the Fixed Numbers of Personnel Administrative Organs'.
6. J. Halligan and M. Turner, *Profiles of Government Administration in Asia* (Canberra: Australian Government Publishing Service, 1995): 173-4.
7. Ibid. 31.
8. Interview, Personnel Administration Branch, 15 July 1997.
9. This word means 'getting rid of rule by cronies'.
10. Acronym for 'Public Services for the Twenty-first Century'.
11. Chalmers Johnson, *Japan: Who Governs? The Rise of the Developmental State* (New York: Norton, 1995): 29.
12. Lam Tao-chiu and Chan Hon S., 'Reforming China's Cadre Management System', *Asian Survey*, 36 (Aug. 1996): 779.
13. These definitions come from X. Zhou, 'Partial Reform and the Chinese Bureaucracy in the Post-Mao Era', *Comparative Political Studies*, 28/3 (1995).
14. D. M. Lampton, 'The Implementation Problem in Post-Mao China', in D. M.

Lampton (ed.), *Policy Implementation in Post-Mao China* (Berkeley and Los Angeles: University of California Press, 1987).

15. Which is very similar to the problem of making administrative changes in Japan— see below.

16. See Geng Yan, *An Introduction to Political and Administrative Reforms in China Since the 1980s* (Hong Kong: Dept. of Public and Social Administration, City University of Hong Kong, 1996) for an overview.

17. See Zhou, 'Partial Reform'.

18. See Lam Tao-chiu and Chan Hon S, 'Reforming China's Cadre Management System', *Asian Survey*, 36 (Aug., 1996).

19. Lam Tao-chiu and Cheung Kai-chee, *The Politics of Administrative Reforms in Post-Mao China*, Conference paper, Public Sector Management Reform in China (Hong Kong Polytechnic University, June 1997).

20. The family registration system (*hukou*) defines where people are allowed to live and is arranged in a hierarchical way according to the status of the town or city. While *hukou* may be purchased, it is unlikely that candidates for civil service exams would have enough money to buy a provincial capital registration.

21. Lam and Chan, 'Reforming China's Cadre Management System': 779.

22. In 1994 and 1996.

23. K. Tashiro, 'The Implications of Small Public Services to National Economic Development: A Case Study of the Japanese Government', in J. P. Burns (ed.), *Asian Civil Service Systems: Improving Efficiency and Productivity* (Singapore: Times Academic Press, 1994).

24. Ryutaro Hashimoto, quoted by Yoko Kobayashi, Reuters News Service, 5 Feb. 1998.

25. Y. Kaneko, *Administrative Reform Efforts in the Government of Japan: Her Experiences and Current Progress* (IIAS Round Table, Quebec City, 14–17 July 1997).

26. Institute of Administrative Management, *Japan's Government Administration at a Glance* (Tokyo: IAM, 1997).

27. Y. Kaneko, *Administrative Reform Efforts in the Government of Japan: Her Experiences and Current Progress*: 13.

28. It was a feature of the US National Performance Review under Al Gore, the French reforms since 1988, for example.

29. *Daily Yomiuri*, 6 Apr. 1997.

30. Partly because he had been convicted of taking a bribe during the Lockheed scandal in 1986 and had received a two-year suspended sentence (*Financial Times*, 13 Sept. 1997).

31. M. O'Uchi, 'A Sensible Analysis of Administrative Reform', in T. Masujima and M. O'Uchi (eds.), *The Management and Reform of the Japanese Government* (Tokyo: Institute of Administrative Management, 1995): 266.

32. U. Suganuma, 'The State Structure Nexus between Japan and China: Are These "Unique", "Mystical" Systems?', *Asian Journal of Public Administration*, 17/2 (1995).

33. Available on IMF's home page at www.imf.org.

34. Foreword to A. Sarji, *Civil Service Reforms*.

35. L. E. Lynn, *New Public Management as an International Phenomenon: A Skeptical View*, Conference Paper, The New Public Management in International Perspective (St Gallen, July 1996).

Conclusions

On 9 December 1998, Dr Kim Kihwan, South Korea's Ambassador for Economic Affairs gave an interview in Sydney,[1] Australia, in which he said that the Korean model of economic development had been a mistake. The combination of large conglomerates and a relatively closed economy had been the cause of Korea's economic crisis. He said:

The chaebol were no accident; they were the result of the government's development strategy. When the government wanted to support a sector of industry, it was administratively inconvenient to deal with many companies. So the policy led to the creation of a chosen few with a protected market and government assistance. Now the government recognizes the need to embrace the market, and the chaebol are now changing.

Dr Kim also said that China was following a policy similar to that of Korea during its rapid growth phase and that this was a mistake. China should, he said, follow Taiwan's model of a more open economy and a more diverse set of companies.

Dr Kim was a prominent member of the governments that implemented the Korean model of economic development and his statement showed the dramatic change in policy that the Kim Dae Jung government had made. While the extent of the changes to the *chaebol* and to government–industry relationships are yet to be seen in practice, it could mark a complete change in the mode of governance of Korea resulting from the crisis. This chapter draws some conclusions about the variety of ways in which the nations of the region are organized in the spheres of the economy, politics, the family, and welfare, and the way in which the state is managed and assesses whether the response to the crisis means an end to the old modes of governance.

Three modes of governance are present in different balances in the countries of the region. The first is derived from the principle that relationships are based on values and ethical rules that are in turn based on position. The position might be in a family, in a geographical area, an accepted system of hierarchy or a system of equality. The rules are known and accepted by the members and they govern decisions and behaviour. Such a mode of governance has been given different names in different times and places since

Confucius and Aristotle and in this book it has been called rule by connections.

The second is the idea of rule by a combination of market principles and some form of competition for power within a framework of law. Relationships between people are mainly based on market exchange in which people engage for individual advantage. While such exchanges may be between equals or between more and less powerful players, the market and a framework of law govern the exchange. The parties to the exchange do not bring to it decision rules and ethical principles based on their relationship outside the exchange. This mode is rule by market.

The third mode is rule by force. Relationships are based on power backed by economic strength, control of institutions, or physical force. Elites rule by gaining control of land, capital, and arms and impose their will on others by coercion. They may engage in economic and political transactions but these are always conducted within an unequal power relationship.

In practice the three modes of governance operate simultaneously. Countries ruled by military dictatorships have markets and may even hold elections for local and national assemblies. Countries that seem to be ruled by markets and elections may in practice be dominated by family connections. Networks of family connections operate within markets. The three principles may even be in balance: there may be free markets operating in most sectors of the economy, a hierarchy which is not contested by those at the lower end, and coercion kept in the background. The idea that states are converging on a 'liberal democratic' model expresses a change in the balance between the three modes of governance, connections, market, and force. If we take the Korean example, the transition from military rule to civilian rule and from a directed economy to a market economy and the decline in importance of the dominant families represent a shift in the balance. It is not (yet) the case that rule by connections has disappeared since the *chaebol* still dominate the economy and the *chaebol* are still largely family run, but the process of reducing their dominance has begun. Nor is it the case that the forces of coercion are permanently confined to barracks as the responses to workers' demonstrations show, but an outright military coup seems unlikely to succeed again.

The question is: how is the balance among the three modes of governance changing and what is the impact of the changes? First, the chapter reviews the main features of the economy, politics, labour, and welfare, and management of government we find operating according to the three modes and how the modes are applied in the region. Then it looks at how changes in the governance rules have been made in recent years and at the implications of these shifts for economic growth and stability.

ECONOMY

According to cultural theories of economic development, the replacement of traditional relationships based on kinship by more 'objective' relationships was an essential part of economic development and modernization. Decisions based on risk and return and prices based on competition were essential elements of a resource allocation system designed to produce optimal results and fastest growth. Obligations of kinship or geography or caste simply get in the way of such a mechanism and therefore produce suboptimal results. While the cultural arguments for slow economic development have now become unpopular, mainly because so many economies which clearly had strong kinship relationships outperformed economies without, the argument has returned in the guise of objections to 'cronyism' in investment decisions and business relationships in general. Buying, selling, lending, and investing among 'cronies' is said to be less efficient than the same transactions among strangers making their decisions on economic criteria and full information disclosure. The same argument applies to investment decisions in an economy governed by force. Powerful states that control resource allocation and make decisions by a planning process designed to benefit the élites are said to make investment decisions less efficiently than markets.

Apart from this rather abstract argument about the merits of the unseen hand of the market being better than other forms of economic governance,[2] there are other differences that arise from alternative balances of market, connections, and force. The fundamental difference is the goals of the corporations and governments engaged in economic decision-making. In a mostly market system there is a greater emphasis on stockholders' wealth, on return on assets, and on stock prices. Fund managers put pressure on managers to make the most profitable use of assets and monitor their performance over very short periods. Decisions on investments and divestments tend to be made on criteria of short-term profitability.

This contrasts with the goals of most Japanese and some Korean corporations during those countries' period of fast growth. The main goal was market share and time-horizons were very long. Managers were expected to grow their companies and hand them over to the next generation of managers in a better state than when they started work there. In the case of Japan, market share could be gained by using profits made at home to subsidize prices in export markets until the competitors gave up. In the later case of the Korean corporations, market share could be 'bought' in the same way but using borrowings rather than profits for the period of price competition. The main reason that these strategies were possible was that stockholders were not demanding large early returns. In many cases the businesses were family owned and family managed, so there was no potential conflict between managers and owners. To some extent, the goals of company size and world market share were linked to the idea of national development and nation building.

What is good for the family is good for the company and is also good for the nation. Of course, such strategies were not always successful, as in the case of Kia motors or other nations' motor car industry plans, or Indonesia's aircraft industry plans. However, there is a strong link between the principle of rule by market and the pressure on short-term profitability and the longer-term goals found where rule by connections is in place. If at the same time there are strong elements of rule by force, long-term strategies can be pursued even more strongly. Projects such as the creation of the Korean shipbuilding industry or the building of the Three Gorges dam in China are more likely when there is powerful government.

In economies where there is a strong emphasis on rule by connection there is a very weak 'market for corporate control' or active mergers and acquisition activity and frequent replacement of management teams and chief executive officers. It was striking that when the Korean government decided to try to clean up corruption at the top of the big corporations it was forced to let the CEOs out of prison quickly to stop their companies and the economy collapsing.

The employment relationship is also different in economies ruled by markets and economies ruled by connections or by force. We saw in Chapter 6 that in some Japanese and Korean companies and in the Chinese SOEs the employment relationship was one of mutual obligations. In the case of China, the direction of labour to jobs was also possible because of the powerful party-state, although jobs were often handed down from one generation to the next in families. The competition that arises from a switch to rule by market makes such obligations less possible as keeping workers employed during periods of slack demand affects the bottom line.

The use of bribery and attitudes to such practices also varies according to the type of rule. People who are used to working in markets where price and quality are the main determinant of who wins business find it difficult and sometimes distasteful to work in markets in which influence is a commodity. Surveys in the FEER regularly report that executives believe that corrupt practices are a barrier to economic progress in the region. For those used to working in an economy ruled by connections, there is not much difference between mutuality accompanied by the exchange of gifts and bribery. Of course, such exchanges distort the economy as decisions are made on the basis of who pays the most but in a sense this is simply a market for influence. It is not different in principle from any other market. It is only very inefficient if every transaction has to be accompanied by a bribe, in which case the bribe becomes a tax on the whole economy. This is most prevalent when there is rule by force and the ruling élite has to be bribed before any transaction can take place.

Market structure also varies according to the mode of rule. Powerful states can create and maintain monopolies and have done for centuries in commodities such as salt, alcohol, or tobacco. Before the economic reform period the Chinese party-state had a virtual monopoly in everything. Other examples of a less complete kind include the Suharto cloves monopoly in Indonesia or the beer monopoly in Taiwan. Rule by connections has tended to create large groups rather than monopolies in the cases of Japan and Korea. In Japan MITI's policy during the developmental state period was to create competition in the home market to make companies strong to compete in overseas markets. The *chaebol* were developed in Korea through alliances between companies, banks, and government to create large, world-competitive businesses. The practice was not universal. Neither Taiwan nor Hong Kong has had government- and bank-sponsored conglomerates. The government of the PRC has sometimes tried to sponsor the growth of large conglomerates on Korean lines. As a generalization it could be said that strong government involvement in the development of industry would tend to produce an economy with a small number of large companies in each sector in which the government takes investment decisions.

Some commentators[3] have suggested that strong family control militates against the growth of very large corporations as families have limited capacity to control their businesses and reach a size limit. To grow further, the families would have to employ directors from outside the family and set up different systems of decision-making and control to take account of the low trust relationship they would have with strangers. While this may be true of some Taiwan and Hong Kong companies it does not seem to be universally true in the region. Rule by market does not necessarily lead to a competitive market structure with many companies in each industry unless there is also a strong anti-trust law.

POLITICS

As we saw in Chapter 5 the liberal-democratic idea is that rule by market and democracy go together and reinforce each other and we have seen that in the cases of Taiwan and Korea at least there has been a combination of market liberalization and democratic elections of national assemblies and presidents. We also saw that there was not a strong link between democracy and resilience in the face of the financial crisis. There is a variety of regime types in the region from democratic to varying degrees of authoritarianism. In the political sphere there are no longer examples of complete rule by force with no element of rule by connection or some of the features normally associated with democracy.

In a democracy we would expect to see political parties contesting for control of some form of national assembly and government. The parties might be expected to represent different coalitions of interests, whether economic groupings such as workers, business owners, farmers, traders, or geographical or in some cases ethnic groups. Political parties take different forms in the different countries. In Taiwan, the opposition to the KMT is partly defined by its attitude towards independence from the PRC. Since the suppression of the Communist Party in Malaysia, politics is largely organized on ethnic and regional lines. The growth of political parties in Indonesia in preparation for the 1999 elections was based partly on personal support for individuals and partly on parties' stance towards Islam. Politics in Hong Kong is based in part on attitudes towards the relationship between Hong Kong and the PRC government. In Korea the opposition which came to power with the election of Kim Dae Jung was closer to the idea of a party representing an identifiable economic interest, that of workers and small businesses as opposed to the large industrial conglomerates.

When political parties are fragmented, governments formed from the winning party cannot make the obvious policy pay-offs to their supporters that they can when the social base of their support is clear. It is more likely that parties will find ways of rewarding a multitude of individual interests and maintain networks of supporters centred on individual representatives or members of the government. The only alternative is an appeal to nationalism, national unity, and the national interest rather than class or fractional interests.

In those cases where political parties are not formed around an identifiable class or social groupings, we would expect the political process to develop within a mode of governance based on connections. Support for political parties would be based on the personal connections of the candidates and their families. We should also not be surprised if the gift relationship or other forms of patronage maintained such connections. None of this is exclusive to Asian societies, of course. Campaign contributions by corporations to political parties in exchange for favourable treatment are a common feature in many Western political systems.

Even where the balance of modes of governance is weighted towards rule by force, there are some features of other modes. In the PRC, where elections to the Party Congress are tightly controlled, there are policy pay-offs to ward off strong dissent and maintain support. This is especially apparent in the policy towards those suffering from the effects of economic restructuring but it also applies to provinces and regions whose support is necessary for the healthy survival of the national government. The maintenance of networks of connections through policy pay-offs is a necessary complement to rule by force.

When the dominant mode of governance is rule by connections, politics takes on distinctive characteristics. While practices vary in detail, the common features seem to be the generation of personal support, the use of patronage to maintain networks of supporters, and the requirement to expand networks to take account of increasingly important groups. If this is the case, and the dominant mode of governance is to be rule by connections, then we should expect the politics of the region to develop into a form of corporatism through which opposing interests are combined to support the ruling party or coalition of parties. This implies that democratization does not necessarily bring an end to rule by connections. It may apply a brake to authoritarian rule but the political processes involved in a democracy lend themselves to the use of network connections. The strong shift away from openly authoritarian politics in some of the countries in the region does not necessarily imply that there will be democratic rule without recourse to the methods of rule by connection that were in place during the periods of rule by force.

LABOUR AND WELFARE

In a market mode of governance, individualism is dominant. The labour market is the main vehicle for most people to take care of their own economic needs and those of their immediate families. If there is to be collectivization or pooling of risk, then there will be a market for insurance and savings schemes. The labour market itself is individualistic and based on single transactions between employers and employees. At the same time, in Western countries that are mainly ruled through the market there is also a connection between welfare and other rights and citizenship. Residual state help in times of sickness and unemployment is a right available to those with citizenship.

We saw in Chapter 6 that the experience of the countries in the region was not the same as this Western model of labour market and welfare. On the one hand, labour market practices have in some cases and for some workers not been a purely economic exchange. On the other hand, the rights to welfare as a result of citizenship vary from strong rights in Japan to weak ones in the Philippines, Indonesia, and Malaysia.

In a force mode of governance there may be direction of labour, operated either through physical force or by creating circumstances in which workers have few or no choices. There have been periods where military force has been more prominent, in Indonesia, during the 1970s in Korea, and in response to demonstrations by workers in the PRC objecting to lay-offs and non-payment. Overt use of force in the field of employee–employer relationships is now less common.

The labour market is modified in circumstances of rule by connections. We saw in Chapter 6 that the employment relationship can be more like a kinship than a market transaction. Within the pseudo-kinship relationship rights and obligations are derived from position as employer or employee rather than from citizenship or from law. It is apparent that when the market becomes dominant, these positional obligations have less importance and rights and obligations disappear. When this happens, mainly because of competition and an increased emphasis on return on assets, the balance can either shift towards rule by market modified by a new system of obligations derived from citizenship rights for workers or rule by market backed by rule by force. What we have seen is that in the PRC the government is trying to establish insurance systems to back up the move to rule by market. In Indonesia in late 1998 there was a strengthening of the civilian militia in response to workers' protests.[4]

The degree of state involvement in welfare seems to be little dependent on the mode of governance. Singapore has probably the greatest involvement, especially if the activities of the CPF are taken into account, and has one of the strongest examples of rule by force. Hong Kong has a combination of rule by market and rule by connections and has a very well-developed public provision in housing, education, and healthcare. Taiwan developed its social provision during a very authoritarian period.

The main effect of governance mode on individual welfare is through its impact on the employment relationship and the degree to which labour is simply treated as a commodity or whether the employment relationship expresses more than that and establishes obligations that look like expressive ties. Welfare systems are developing in response to these changes in the labour market. The systems are mostly based on an insurance principle and employers and employees make contributions. These schemes share the risk of periods of sickness although there is little development of insurance for periods of unemployment as yet. If the economies of the region are to be exposed to the big fluctuations in employment and incomes they experienced during the 1997/8 crisis, individuals will be exposed to greater and greater risks. Whereas in the past the tendency has been for the risk to be shared by the employees and their individual employer, as firms become more subject to short-term stockholder pressure it is likely that in future the insurance principle will be detached from the employment relationship. Employers may be forced to make contributions to a fund as part of the wage cost but they are unlikely to be responsible for managing the funds. The degree of state involvement in the collective arrangements is likely to vary with local politics.

MANAGING THE STATE

It was clear in Chapter 7 that shifting the management processes of governments from those based on connections or the use of hierarchical power to those based on market-type mechanisms was difficult because of the beliefs and material interests served by the old ways. In circumstances of rule by force, civil servants have their patrons in the ruling élites and the military and in turn exercise patronage in issuing contracts, licences, and permissions. In a system of rule by connections, members of families whose relatives occupy other important positions in society will staff the upper reaches of the civil service.

The idea of the developmental state which some observers saw in Japan and to a lesser extent in Korea was that of a dispassionate, technocratic civil service élite who were well paid and not subject to 'rent-seeking' behaviour. They could act in the national interest, distinct from individual, factional, or sectoral interests. To maintain their independence, recruitment had to be done through competitive examinations in which family and other connections would be overruled by merit. Before the 1997/8 crisis other governments, including the Malaysian, looked to this model to enhance their economic development capability. While such a dispassionate technocracy may have existed during the early growth period, what the crisis seemed to show was that sufficient connections between civil servants and banks and businesses were revealed to cast doubt on the model. Despite the difficulties, many countries' civil services are being 'modernized' in an effort to establish labour markets and bureaucracies that operate according to performance rather than connections.

AFTER RULE BY FORCE AND RULE BY CONNECTIONS?

In each sphere, it seems that the modes of governance are changing in the region. The Japanese and other governments are trying to change the financial systems so that markets operate rather than connections. Korea's government is reigning back the *chaebol* and opening up the economy to international investment and competition. The PRC government is removing the protection of the SOEs that has been in place since they were established after the revolution. The Indonesian government has made noises about breaking up the family-based industries and monopolies of the previous ruling family. Labour markets are becoming less an expression of obligational ties between employers and employees and more a market exchange. Workers and governments are making arrangements for pensions and other welfare needs outside the employment relationships.

Kim Dae Jung, president of Korea, describes the changes in his country as being a response to 'universal globalism'.[5] Not only was the exposure of Korea to competition and investment from overseas inevitable because of globalization, it was good for the long-term health of the economy and was a useful spur to internal economic and social reforms.

Whether the economies are converging on a free-market mode of governance or not, they have developed distinctive institutional arrangements. If generalization is possible, there are four patterns.

One is of very strong connections between government, financial institutions, and industry. Growth was directed to some extent, particular sectors being backed as likely successes and risk was shared and reduced by the state being the underwriter of investments and loans. The selected sectors benefited from protection by tariffs and non-tariff barriers to imports and could develop profits in home markets that could be used to finance entry into export markets. Foreign direct investment was controlled by regulations about the proportion of domestic businesses that could be owned by foreigners. Not all the chosen sectors would be successful and some investments would be wasted, but in general such an institutional arrangement did produce fast growth and economic transformations especially in Japan and Korea. To some extent this approach was also followed in Malaysia. The prerequisites for this mode were that domestic savers would entrust their savings to financial intermediaries (banks and other institutions) involved in the investments and loans, and there had to be sufficient overlap of membership of the sectors government, finance, and industry for the money to be channelled in the planned direction and not be diverted by a large number of independent intermediaries making purely market-based investment decisions. The mode of governance is mainly one of rule by connections.

The second model is of government-backed industrial growth that relied mainly on foreign direct investment supported by government-financed infrastructure and attractive tax regimes and labour laws. Most growth would take place in export-processing zones occupied by foreign-owned plants. The prerequisites for this model are that labour costs and therefore the level of economic development of the industrial workforce should be kept down to competitive levels, since by definition the investment decisions are labour-cost-sensitive, and domestic producers should be compensated to some extent for the special treatment of foreigners if they are to maintain their support for government. Thailand and the Philippines have followed this approach to some extent. The mode of governance is rule by market backed by rule by force.

China is probably a case on its own. The post-Mao economic reforms retained a strong element of government planning and party-state control. There were strong connections between banks and industry, to such an extent that the banks are hardly recognizable as banks. Foreign direct investment is encouraged but tightly controlled and much of it benefits from being from 'Greater China' in which family and province connections can provide a degree of trust and stability which would be absent in purely market transactions. Bribery and the exchange of gifts have been an important if officially disapproved part of the network-building activity. Regulations are in place to prevent instability, including breaks on trading if there is too great a fluctuation on the Shanghai and Shenzhen Stock Exchanges and a strong control over the exchange rate. The mode of governance is mainly rule by connections with an increasing element of rule by market.

Taiwan, Hong Kong, and Singapore exemplify a fourth case. Here there are strong governments ruling during the growth periods without much democratic accountability, able to develop infrastructure and labour laws but unwilling to intervene in the details of investment decisions. Domestic businesses get what support they need from government but there is some distinction between the people who run businesses and the people who run the government. There might be some government preference for sectors and some government support for them, such as the development of port facilities in Singapore and Hong Kong or encouraging electronics in Taiwan. The economies are also opportunistic, businesses changing products and markets to meet market changes. In cases of potential instability all three have the possibility of a residual rule by force, but the main mode of governance has been a combination of market and connections.

This classification has omitted the 'kleptocracies' of Indonesia under Suharto and the Philippines under the Marcos regime. Dominance by a family and their close supporters backed by the military is a mode of governance that falls between rule by connection and rule by force and has come under attack by those who fall outside the network of connections.

In each case the impact of a change in the balance of mode of governance will be different. In the first model in which investment has been directed and the distinction between government and finance and business has been blurred, there is a wide range of reforms to be carried out before the balance is tipped towards rule by markets. First, risk is increased. Investment decisions would no longer have the implicit or explicit backing of the government. Funds will be harder and more expensive to raise. The opening of the economies to a higher degree of foreign portfolio investment has already brought greater volatility to equity markets as the connections between manufacturing and finance are loosened. The 'disciplines' of the market imposed by more powerful investment groups are very different from the mutuality implied by the older networks of connections.

Will the changes that have started in Japan and Korea lead to slower growth? In the case of Japan growth has already slowed for the past decade as companies have moved production overseas and as costs in Japan have risen with the standard of living. Growth will only benefit from the liberalization that is taking place if companies find ways of improving their productivity and quality even further. The only difference will be that the pressure for improvement will no longer come from the old motivation of 'national' achievement and growth through growth in market share, but will be spurred by stock prices, dividends, and the market for corporate control implied by an active investment community operating globally. In Korea the change is likely to lead to fewer heroic and misplaced investment decisions such as the Samsung carmaking venture that was undertaken at a time of world overcapacity in carmaking. On the other hand, had the changes come earlier, they might have meant that many of the industries in which Korean companies are world leaders would never have existed.

An alternative to Kim Dae Jung's view that a positive and open response to globalization is the only way out for the Korean economy is that it was too much exposure to foreign investors that caused its problems. After all, balance sheets with very high debt/equity ratios are a problem only if they cause stockholders to sell. Bad debts only become a problem when they are called in. Once all such transactions are kept within a closed circle, debt-financed expansion is still an option. Openness might simply expose all companies to the same problems. Kim's solution, that the big groups should divest and that they should clean up their balance sheets by swapping debt for equity, and that the banks should lend on more commercial criteria, will certainly bring Korea into line with those parts of the world where investors are separate from managers. Whether this will lead to economic recovery remains to be seen.

Governments operating the second mode, rule by market backed by force, have no pressure to transform. They are the ideal-type of market economy including low taxes and a cheap labour force. They are limited in their growth prospects to those industries, whether financed domestically or by foreign investment, where labour cost is an important factor. Recent experience of the collapse of world prices of memory chips[6] and the vagaries of the world market for sports shoes have shown that very heavy dependency on exports and low-cost production makes any country's manufacturing industry very vulnerable to world markets and cost changes. Where there is pressure for change it is to make markets more dominant, as in the banking sector in Thailand where the government has already changed the rules to allow more foreign ownership.

Apparently the PRC began a long process of a move towards rule by market in 1978. Currently rule by connections and its impact on the economy are still apparent. There are still bureaucratic procedures for permissions and licences for domestic and foreign investments that require *guanxi* in its various forms before development can take place. While this may slow development as companies spend large amounts of money at the beginning of a project to simply put the permissions and connections in place, it also leads to spectacular developments which might not have been put in place under a system of rule by markets. Property development is a case in which overoptimism has led to overprovision of, for example, office and luxury residential space in Shanghai and hotel space in Beijing. These are the exceptions: the combination of close links between government finance and industry and the ability to channel both domestic savings and foreign investment have produced in the coastal cities of China the fastest and longest growth the world has seen. Such connections have been blamed for the slow growth in Japan since 1989 but there is no obvious sign that they have damaged China's growth. Some stresses are beginning to show in the financial sector. While definitions and disclosure of bad debts in China are not comparable with elsewhere there is clearly a debt problem. SOEs have been financing their wage bills with borrowings and have incurred debts they are unlikely to repay. The government has taken a very public stance on the financial sector by closing one troubled non-bank financial institution.[7]

What is the reason for further economic liberalization? One is the desire to apply to join the WTO. Liberalization of import controls, especially on computers, would be a necessary condition of membership, which may in turn be a necessary move to avoid further restrictions on Chinese imports to the USA. Looser import controls would mean more competition for Chinese manufacturers and therefore a need for a more liberal regime in which to compete. The second is a desire by the government to develop domestic service industries as a complement to the manufacturing growth. As in manufacturing, there will be pressure from WTO membership to liberalize the service sector.

While liberalization of imports into China will no doubt gradually develop, it is hard to imagine the breakdown of the network of connections between the party-state and finance and business. Even more difficult to imagine is a similar development in the political sphere to allow independent competing parties to stand in free elections for the Party Congress and Central Committee. That is not to say that the party-state is unwilling to see the development of private business and various forms of collective businesses in the TVE sector, nor that it will revert to production quotas and fixed prices. It does suggest though that China will continue to have a distinctive mode of governance in which connections, organized through the party, are the dominant organizing mechanism and in which the use of force will remain not too far in the background to maintain the regime.

STABILITY

To what extent will the changes in mode of governance affect economic and political stability? The riots in Indonesia have been an illustration of the impact of economic instability on the lives of working people. Big increases in unemployment and decreases in living standards have been the result of the financial crisis. UNICEF[8] has reported that in Thailand the unemployment and low pay resulting from the crisis have resulted in 5 million children being withdrawn from school because their parents cannot pay the fees. There are frequent reports of workers' demonstrations in Korea and the PRC. Once prosperity recedes people can no longer be relied on to be passive or compliant.

Is such instability inevitable? If there has been a change in governance towards a more open market system, does this mean that there will be frequent oscillations between high growth rates and declines in output? The 1997/8 crisis brought instability in two ways: exchange rate falls meant that dollar profits from exports collapsed even when volumes were maintained, as the value of exports in dollars fell. As stock and property prices collapsed, people holding those assets spent less, investment fell, and there was an accelerated recession. The recessions lasted longer than they might have done as a result of high-interest rates and tight fiscal policy in those countries that borrowed from the IMF and accepted its policy prescriptions.

To what extent could such a cyclical decline be avoided? Clearly some control over short-term flows of capital into and out of currencies and stock markets would avoid sudden sharp price changes and there is currently a discussion among the international institutions about the possible arrangements for controls. This would alleviate the results of the herd-type panics that were described in Chapter 1.

In the longer term it should be the case that currency, property, and stock markets are based on economic reality and that speculative booms and busts are variations around underlying values. The crisis was set off at least in part by concerns about profit and sales growth declining and about the balance sheets of certain companies in the region. The remaining question is whether it is necessary to shift from rule by connections to rule by markets to correct those concerns and make profitable companies that would not be subject to such big variations in performance.

Rule by connections brings stability in capital and labour markets. When stockholders have a familial relationship with the companies in which they hold stocks they will not sell them when profitability dips. This will be the case in family-owned businesses and in those where employee stockholders also have a family-type relationship with the employer. The same applies to a familial employment relationship in which employees are not necessarily laid off when sales drop. Close relationships between banks and corporations also seem to have the effect of tolerance of periods of losses or non-payment of debts. These features of rule by connections reduce the volatility of markets and the amplitude of economic cycles.

A further source of instability in the change in emphasis in governance mode is imbalance among the economic, political, and social spheres. Liberalization in the economic sphere can lead to the development of new classes of people, especially a growing urban working class and a new middle class. While the evidence in Chapter 5 was that these new classes do not necessarily demand the features of a liberal democracy, such as the right to elect political parties, these classes do have demands. They are likely to de disconnected from the ruling networks and therefore excluded from the benefits of membership. This is most stark in the PRC where migrants to the cities do not have the rights that come from urban residence status but it also applies elsewhere to access to land for housing and to élite education.

Liberalization in the political sphere can bring political processes that are not matched in the economic. The advent of democracy in Korea produced successful politicians who opposed the rule by connections of the ruling families. Kim's actions against the *chaebol* can be interpreted not simply as resulting from an ideological commitment to markets and openness but also as a way of getting economic power away from the old ruling class.

The most obvious imbalance occurs when rule by market becomes the norm in labour markets but familistic connections are in place in the sphere of welfare. While migrants to the urban areas make great efforts to support their families who may be elsewhere, it is not always possible for their earnings to support access to healthcare and education for their families. The serious unemployment in the region that resulted from the crisis showed how vulnerable workers and their families were.

One aspect of the shift in balance of modes of governance is the nature and role of the law. Rule by force and rule by connections both have their own ethics. Dictators rarely need recourse to law or an independent legal system. The ethics of relationships also do not require the rule of law: virtue or obligations are defined in the relationships and do not need to be defined by anyone outside the relationship. Once rule by connections is replaced by rule by market, a framework of law is required.

There are two sets of circumstances in which a switch from rule by connections to rule by markets can produce instability that can only be avoided by laws and regulations. The first is when the members of the connected network start to break the ethical rules implied in the relationships, when self-interest takes over from mutuality. Once the 'relational ethics' have broken down, unless they are replaced by some other rules backed by a legal system, markets will be chaotic. The second circumstance is when dealings are extended beyond the network to strangers.

The example of the *tobashi* deals in Japan illustrates the point: it was perfectly ethical for a stockbroker to protect a client from losses because such protection was implied by a stockbroker–client relationship within the network of connections. Once clients from outside the connections also deal with the broker and do not have the benefit of the protection, there are no universally applicable rules derived from the relationship. Regulation by rules or by law is required to allow this market to operate to the satisfaction of the clients outside the network. This applies also to banking rules, accounting and disclosure practices, and trading rules in markets.

This is the root of the IMF interventions in the region. If strangers (foreigners) are to invest and trade in the area, they do not want to be treated differently from the locals: because they have no connections to govern their transactions they need rule by markets supported by legal and accounting frameworks that they can trust. But it is unlikely that the whole region will switch completely from rule by connections to rule by markets. The networks of family and other connections that stretch both within nations and across national boundaries have organized successful businesses that survived the crisis. What is likely to happen is that there will be a shift in the balance of governance from rule by connections to rule by market. There will still be cultural differences between businesses in Asia and businesses in the West and only exposure to outside investors will bring pressure on managers to produce short-term returns and save their businesses from acquisitions.

GLOBAL MARKET RULES?

A strong version of the globalization argument would be that every territory in the world is joined in a world set of connections. In the absence of a world government and a world set of expressive ties the form of these connections is the market. Free flows of goods and capital, although not of labour, will be strong enough to establish world market prices and world levels of taxation. Any attempt at protection from these world tendencies, whether by nation states or groups of states in trading blocs, will result in retaliation from the other market players and in the impoverishment of those trying to protect themselves.

The idea of a nation, in economic terms, is incompatible with this version of globalization. National interest is opposed to the economic rationalism and dispassionate instrumental relationships in a market. The idea of national interest, combining the interests of all classes in a society, is incompatible with belief in the power of market forces. A global market should produce a stateless world élite operating in world markets and with allegiance only to themselves. If there are nations, they should exist only for administrative convenience or perhaps to satisfy the residual feelings of belonging among those who do not feel that they belong only to the global market. Differences among geographical entities would eventually disappear as market rules apply universally. Ethical standards arising from cultural definitions of relationships would give way to the rules of the market. Strangers would be treated no differently from family. Obligations would exist only in a contractual sense.

How likely is such a strong version of globalization to be played out in Asia? First, the idea of connections extending from the family to the nation is strong and continues to be promoted by governments. Even ethnically mixed nations such as Malaysia and the Philippines manage to sustain a sense of national identity, not to mention the stronger cases of Japan, China, and Korea. The economic and political élites of the nations of the area are mainly rooted in their home territories. Despite the economic expansionism of Japanese and later Korean overseas investment, the corporations in those countries are still mainly run from the home territory, rather than a mobile élite of stateless managers. The home base still provides a certain amount of protection and support from governments and a local network of trading and financial partnerships. The flows of capital around the world are large compared with any nation's investment but FDI does not dominate national economies and most investments are still mostly made using local savings. The exception may be the PRC whose nationhood's boundaries were stretched into Greater China for the purposes of capital flows. The reunification of China and Hong Kong corrected one of the anomalies of national boundaries and investments and put the Hong Kong investments in China within the national boundary. In the region, national élites have not abandoned their home bases and become global.

Second, as this book has shown, there are still many elements of rule by connections in the region and those who benefit from being part of the network of connections within each country will maintain their privileges rather than abandon them to world competition. Sometimes international changes or local changes in power may force them to. No doubt membership of the WTO will have an impact on some members of the ruling networks in the PRC and Taiwan. Factional conflicts will harm some parts of national élites more than others as power struggles progress in Korea and Indonesia, for example. But the idea of national networks giving up their connections in favour of market relationships that could include anybody in the world who wants to participate in the market is far-fetched.

Third, a true world market with world prices would require much more freedom of migration than currently exists. While there is migration in the region from poorer to richer countries, the flows are not sufficient to equalize income levels. While controls on migration are not primarily in place to protect local income levels, that is one of their effects. In many cases the producers of local services will be able to maintain their living standards without fear of their jobs being given to migrants.

Fourth, political struggles and argument are still conducted at national level and political parties and trade unions are almost all national, albeit with international connections. The resolution of those struggles needs to be made at the level of the nation. It was clear in the review of welfare policies that national politics and bargaining have been a source of national differences. These bargaining processes are mediated through political institutions and it is unlikely that global institutions will be created to handle them.

For these reasons it is unlikely that the world market or the supranational institutions will replace national governments and all the elements of rule by connections. The crisis of 1997/8 did shake the confidence of governments in the region, however, and showed the power of the financial markets. There is no doubt that in the sphere of economic policy it marked a shift in the balance towards rule by market, along with a relaxation in the rules about openness to foreign investment and about financial disclosure. At the same time it revealed the destructive power of unregulated markets and currency and stock speculation and the inability of any supranational institution to counter the causes of speculation at an international level or correct their effects at national level.

If it is true that there will be a shift in the balance between rule by connections and rule by market at national level, the implication is that the ethics of rule by connection will have to be replaced by adequate rules for those markets to operate. Some of these are already being put in place in areas such as banking and stock-market regulations. Discussions have only started about establishing some rules at the international level for the operation of stock and currency markets. The WTO's mission of removing barriers to trade in goods and increasingly in services is continuing and so far changes in rules about capital and financial flows have been about removing barriers and conditions on investments. If the extreme damage caused to millions of people by the 1997/8 crash is to be avoided in future, some limits will have to put on the power of the markets. Since the international institutions are still dominated by liberal pro-marketeers, such a prospect is unlikely.

NOTES

1. *Australian Financial Review*, 9 Dec. 1998, p. 8.
2. The argument goes back to, and beyond, Adam Smith.
3. e.g. F. Fukuyama, 'Confucianism and Democracy', *Journal of Democracy*, 6/2 (1995).
4. In November 1998 125,000 civilian vigilantes were deployed to back up security

forces in Jakarta to secure the 'special session' of parliament, but were withdrawn after protests by human rights groups and the lynching of four members of the paramilitary squads. *Sydney Morning Herald*, 9 Dec. 1998.

5. Article in *Korea Times*, 5 Nov. 1998.
6. Dynamic random access memory prices on global markets continued to fall in 1998. Prices of 64 megabit DRAMS dropped to around nine dollars from around 14 to 15 dollars at the beginning of the year, while prices of 16 megabit DRAMS dropped to around 1.5 to 1.8 dollars from about 10 dollars in 1997. Xinhua News Agency, 8 Dec. 1998.
7. Guangdong International Trust and Investment Corp (Gitic).
8. Xinhua News Agency news bulletin, 8 Dec. 1998.

INDEX